ON HIS MA~~

Your
Ration Book

Issued to safeguard your food supply

HOLDER'S NAME AND REGISTERED ADDRESS

COMPARE WITH YOUR IDENTITY
CARD AND REPORT ANY
DIFFERENCE TO YOUR FOOD
OFFICE

DO NOT ALTER

Surname *Cherish*

Other Names *Gabriel N.*

Address *Molyneux House*

Carlton Hill London

NAT. REG. NO.	8 AWH	692	1

Date of Issue **- 7 JUL 1941**   Serial Number of Book

If found, please return to   **PT**

CITY OF WESTMINSTER.
FOOD OFFICE.

R.B. [General] 1

The Blitz
A Very
Peculiar
History

With NO added doodlebugs

'London can take it!'
*Title of upbeat Ministry of Information
film about the Blitz*

In memory of my
Grandma, with thanks
DA

Additional artwork: Carolyn Franklin (p. 128)
Editor: Stephen Haynes

Published in Great Britain in MMX by
Book House, an imprint of
The Salariya Book Company Ltd
25 Marlborough Place, Brighton BN1 1UB
www.salariya.com
www.book-house.co.uk

HB ISBN-13: 978-1-907184-18-5

> **WARNING:** The Salariya Book Company accepts
> no responsibility for the historical recipes in this
> book. They are included only for their historical
> interest and may not be suitable for modern use.

1 3 5 7 9 8 6 4 2
A CIP catalogue record for this book is available
from the British Library.
Printed and bound in Dubai.
Printed on paper from sustainable sources.

The Blitz
A Very Peculiar History

With NO added doodlebugs

Written by
David Arscott

Illustrated by
David Antram

Created and designed by
David Salariya

and
Mark Bergin

'What a piece of dirty brutality in plan and in deed. As warfare it will not work. It will merely fan the flame of righteous hate in every British heart.'
Daily Express leader column

'The thing I shall always remember above all the other things in my life is the monstrous loveliness of that one single view of London on a holiday night – London stabbed with great fires, shaken by explosions, its dark regions along the Thames sparkling with the pin points of white-hot bombs, all of it roofed over with a ceiling of pink that held bursting shells, balloons, flares and the grind of vicious engines.'
War correspondent Ernie Pyle

'Now I can look the East End in the face.'
Queen Elizabeth (later the Queen Mother) after Buckingham Palace was damaged by a German bomb

Contents

Putting the London Blitz on the map

(See page 152 for a map of the Blitz outside London.)

West End

THAMES

RIVER

Key to London landmarks
1. Victoria & Albert Museum
2. Buckingham Palace
3. Westminster Abbey
4. Houses of Parliament
5. National Gallery
6. British Museum
7. St Paul's Cathedral

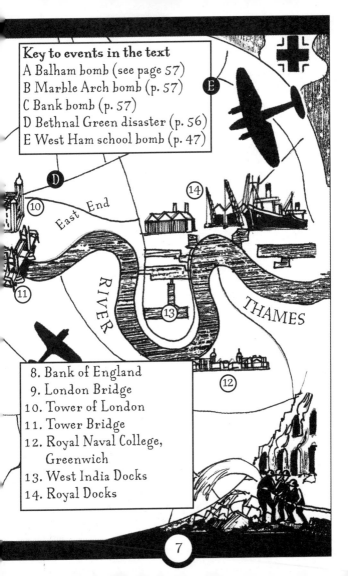

Key to events in the text
A Balham bomb (see page 57)
B Marble Arch bomb (p. 57)
C Bank bomb (p. 57)
D Bethnal Green disaster (p. 56)
E West Ham school bomb (p. 47)

East End

RIVER

THAMES

8. Bank of England
9. London Bridge
10. Tower of London
11. Tower Bridge
12. Royal Naval College, Greenwich
13. West India Docks
14. Royal Docks

For some children, evacuation was a great adventure. Others were not so keen.

INTRODUCTION

Why the bombs fell

Very late one night in the spring of 1944, a toddler unable to sleep was playing by the window of his north London home when his grandmother heard the unmistakable swish of a parachute wafting down through the pitch-black sky with a vicious landmine attached below.

She snatched the child up seconds before the window shattered and sprayed the room with splinters of glass. It was one small incident among thousands, but without her prompt action this book about the grim years of the Blitz would have been written by someone else.

Yes, you guessed it – that toddler was me! It was nothing personal, of course, but when I grew old enough to ask, I wondered why someone was intent on blowing innocent little me (and millons more like me) into even smaller pieces. And I wondered how people like my poor Grandma managed to cope with this kind of thing for year after gruelling year.

Well, the Blitz – from the German *Blitzkrieg*, or 'lightning war' – was every bit as terrible as you might imagine, but (as we shall see) there were lighter moments among the gloom, and the constantly bombarded citizens of London and other British cities found many ingenious methods of coping with it.

Death from the air

It's said that when the first landmines were dropped, many people were killed because they didn't know what they were. Policemen and air-raid wardens ran towards the parachutes, mistaking them for German pilots who had bailed out of their planes.

Chamberlain's bit of paper

Did the war have to happen? In 1938 the British prime minister, Neville Chamberlain, very much hoped he could prevent it. He flew out to meet the German leader Adolf Hitler in Munich, and came back clutching not only his trademark umbrella, but an agreement which, he claimed, promised 'peace for our time'.

The agreement said that:

- Germany, which wanted to expand beyond its borders, could take control of part of Czechoslovakia called the Sudetenland.
- But that was all it could have, and it mustn't go any further.

Many people approved of this agreement ('appeasement', it was called), but wiser heads warned that Hitler was a ruthless man who would only abide by the first part of it – and they were absolutely right.

His army soon took all of Czechoslovakia and then threatened to sweep north into Poland. He wanted to dominate the whole world.

The Kindertransport

Hitler and his Nazi party hated Jews and wanted to exterminate them. In November 1938, 200 German synagogues were destroyed and thousands of Jewish homes and businesses were ransacked in a pogrom – an organised anti-Jewish riot – known as *Kristallnacht*. The name means 'crystal night' or 'night of broken glass', referring to all the shop windows that were broken by the rioters.

Since it was clear that much worse was to come, a rescue scheme known as *Kindertransport* (child transport) was organised. The idea was to bring Jewish children under the age of 17 to safety in Britain from Germany, Austria, Poland and Czechoslovakia.

Around 10,000 of them reached safety, the last train setting out only two days before the outbreak of war. Most of them would never see their parents or any members of their families again, as six million Jews were put to death in the extermination camps.

Some brave people in German-occupied countries tried to protect their Jewish neighbours. In occupied Holland, Anne Frank wrote her famous diary as she and her family hid in an upstairs room for two years before being betrayed. She died of typhus in the Bergen-Belsen concentration camp.

Here are two things Hitler is supposed to have said about the British prime minister after signing the agreement:

• 'Chamberlain seemed such a nice old gentleman that I thought I would give him my autograph.'

• 'If ever that silly old man comes interfering here again with his umbrella, I'll kick him downstairs and jump on his stomach in front of the photographers.'

He jumped on Poland instead. Chamberlain had promised to support the Poles if Hitler attacked them, so Britain declared war on Germany on Sunday 3 September 1939.

The phoney war

The bombing was still a long way off at this stage. In fact, the next seven months were referred to as 'the Phoney War', because there wasn't a German in sight. That gave the British some time to prepare for the worst. Millions of gas masks were handed out, food was rationed and many thousands of sandbags were filled and stacked outside public buildings to protect them from bomb blast.

Meanwhile, Hitler's troops had already overrun Denmark and Norway. Holland, Belgium and France were next in line – and then, inevitably, it would be Britain's turn.

Enter Winnie

At this point Chamberlain furled his umbrella and resigned as prime minister, knowing that too many people had lost confidence in his ability to lead the country against Hitler.

The man who enthusiastically stepped into his shoes was Winston Churchill, who later said that he felt all his previous experiences in life had led him to this dramatic moment.

Churchill was a controversial figure who had made quite a few enemies in the past, yet nobody doubted his ability to organise Britain's armed forces and to inspire the public with his stirring speeches.

British bulldog: Winston Churchill proved to be an inspiring wartime leader.

Ten things to know about
Winston Churchill

1. He was a descendant of another war hero, the first Duke of Marlborough, and was born (in 1874) at Blenheim Palace.

2. As a 10-year-old schoolboy in Sussex, he was stabbed in the chest by a lad whose ear he'd pulled in an argument. Fortunately, it was nothing serious, although the other boy was expelled. (Was this Churchill's first victory?)

3. In his twenties he became a cavalry officer and served in India and Afghanistan before taking part in one of the last British cavalry charges – at the Battle of Omdurman in the Sudan.

4. During the Boer War he worked as a reporter in South Africa for the *Morning Post* newspaper and was captured after bravely helping wounded soldiers to escape on a train. He managed to get away, and reached safety after nine days on the run – becoming an instant celebrity in Britain.

5. He entered Parliament as a Conservative MP, but later switched to the Liberals – and then back to the Conservatives again. This made him quite a few enemies.

6. He was a tremendous public speaker but had trouble pronouncing the letter 's', which always came out like 'sh'.

7. He earned his living by writing dozens of books on history, war and literature. One of these was the massive, four-volume *History of the English-Speaking Peoples* – although he had other people to do a lot of the research for him. He won the Nobel Prize for Literature in 1953.

8. With his American wife Clemmie, he bought a house in Kent called Chartwell, where he relaxed by painting, keeping tropical fish and building brick walls at the rate of 60 bricks an hour. You can visit the house today. He once entered one of his landscape paintings at the prestigious Royal Academy under the false name of Winter – and had it accepted by the jury. (They didn't have a section for brick walls.)

9. Although he held several major political posts at different times, including First Lord of the Admiralty and Chancellor of the Exchequer, he hadn't had a government job for ten years when the Second World War broke out. Some people had regarded him as a dangerous warmonger!

10. He smoked up to ten cigars a day – and rather liked a brandy, too.

Dunkirk

But Churchill had been prime minister for little more than a fortnight when he was faced with a disaster.

In May 1940, British, French and Canadian troops were trapped on the French coast at Dunkirk (Dunkerque), with an awesome German army in front of them and the sea behind. Their situation was so desperate that British king George VI called for a week of prayer throughout the country.

The amazing rescue which followed has given the phrase 'Dunkirk spirit' to the English

language. A vast flotilla of private fishing boats, pleasure cruisers and commercial vessels crossed and re-crossed the English Channel to rescue the stranded soldiers while German bombers unleashed a series of brutal attacks upon them.

Although some 338,000 troops were evacuated, Churchill was quick to point out that the operation was 'a miracle of deliverance' rather than a victory.

- 68,000 men were killed or captured.
- Six destroyers and 177 planes were lost.
- 126 merchant seamen died.

The Battle of Britain

And then a month later, in July 1940, the German offensive began. Hitler's air force, the Luftwaffe, swept in to cripple Britain's defences and so prepare the way for Operation Sea Lion – the invasion of Britain. For week after week – from mid-July to the end of October – it was the heroic resistance of the pilots of RAF Fighter Command which held the planned invasion at bay.

The Spitfire

Though the Hawker Hurricane played a vital role in shooting down Luftwaffe bombers, it was the nippy Spitfire - the fastest plane in the world - that caught the public imagination, as its brave pilots duelled with German 'aces' in one-to-one combat.

Lord Beaverbrook, the *Daily Express* newspaper tycoon, was appointed minister of aircraft production. He made the most of this enthusiasm by launching several clever wheezes that were good for morale:

• 'Pots and pans for Spitfires'
The idea was for householders to bring their surplus aluminium gadgets to collection centres so that they could be turned into the Duralumin used to build aeroplanes.

The salvage dumps were soon overflowing with kettles, pans, tin baths, cigarette boxes and the like - although aluminium wasn't really in short supply.

• Spitfire Funds
The cost of a Spitfire was set at £5,000 (although it was actually more than twice that), and towns and organisations of many kinds set about collecting money for one. Amazingly, some 1,500 were provided in this way - about a sixth of the total produced during the war.

• Wings for Victory Week
There were parades, exhibitions and a government savings scheme which provided funds for new aircraft.

Supermarine Spitfire

Civilians below would look up into the skies of southern England to watch desperate dogfights between Spitfires, Hurricanes and their German counterparts.

The Battle of Britain lasted from July to October 1940. Of the 2,927 Allied pilots who fought, 544 died. Many were sent into the air with only a few hours' training and in patched-up aircraft; their life expectancy was a mere 87 operational hours.

Churchill, as usual, had the words for it:

'Never in the field of human conflict was so much owed by so many to so few.'

Just when the RAF seemed to be at breaking point, Hitler changed his tactics. The fighting in the air had not succeeded in destroying Britain's defences. The next phase of the war would be the heavy bombing of British cities.

The Blitz had begun.

CHAPTER ONE

OPERATION PIED PIPER

It was quite an adventure for a small child to be sent away to the seaside or into the countryside to escape the threat of German bombs. And, very often, it was a pretty dreadful adventure, too!

If you're the kind of person who finds the idea of spending a few days away from home on a school trip a bit of a lonesome experience, imagine what it was like to be packed off to a strange new place without having the foggiest idea when you might be coming back. And who knew *what* you might eventually be coming back to, once the bombs had fallen and destroyed large areas of towns and cities?

The City of Benares

Whisking children away by ship from endangered British cities to the safety of Canada must have seemed a good idea at the time – but why had nobody thought about the menace lurking beneath the Atlantic waves?

In September 1940, 90 evacuee children from the Liverpool area were taken aboard the steam passenger ship *City of Benares* bound for Quebec and Montreal.

The ship was hit by a torpedo fired by an enemy U-boat (submarine), and it sank terrifyingly fast, within half an hour. A total of 248 people were killed, including 77 of the evacuees.

One of the lifeboats, with six young boys on board, drifted away unnoticed and spent all of eight days bobbing about on the sea before being spotted from the air.

Those lads certainly had a tale to tell afterwards – but the overseas evacuation scheme was dropped immediately.

Mothers, send them out of London!
Wartime slogan

The government gave their evacuation scheme the code-name Operation Pied Piper – which is pretty scary when you think about what happened to the children in Hamelin! The bombing hadn't yet begun, but the idea was to get the children away to safety before it did.

There were several waves of evacuations:

• The first began two days before war was declared, and soon 1,500,000 children were uprooted and on the move – but because the bombing didn't start straight away, more than half of them returned within months.

This caused a problem, because many of the schools in London had closed down. With their fathers in the army and their mothers working in a factory, the 'dead-end kids' had nothing to do but roam the streets all day.

• In September 1940 the Blitz started and the dash for safety began all over again. For many children it was a repeat performance.

• In 1944, when the worst seemed to be over, the Germans began firing rockets across the Channel (see page 40), and now another million children, women, elderly and disabled people fled the targeted areas.

This is what you took with you:

Girls
- vest
- pair of knickers
- petticoat
- 2 pairs of stockings
- 6 handkerchiefs
- slip
- blouse
- cardigan

Boys
- 2 vests
- 2 pairs of pants
- pair of trousers
- 2 pairs of socks
- 6 handkerchiefs
- pullover or jersey

> Rats! Mum shouldn't have put that extra pair of socks in.

Of course you were also supposed to keep clean and tidy, so you packed a comb, soap, toothbrush and flannel in your suitcase – or, more likely, your ever-hopeful parent did it for you. *'Do remember to wash behind your ears, dear!'*

You would have had your gas mask, an overcoat, plimsolls (a bit like trainers) and wellington boots among this paraphernalia, too. You were probably exhausted carrying that lot around before you even got to the railway station.

The journey itself could be very frightening. If you were lucky you'd be with a friend, but the train would stop at various stations along the way, and the billeting officers – the people who decided who went where – would come on board and order children off at random.

They weren't always very kind about it, either: 'You – off you get!'

Imagine seeing your best friend whisked off into the evening gloom, while you travelled on alone, with nobody to talk to and not knowing where you'd end up.

And the school went, too

Many children who thought they would be escaping the torture of the classroom were in for a nasty shock, because their teachers accompanied them to their 'reception area' to make sure that they kept up to scratch with their work while they were away.

Mind you, they sometimes had to share buildings (not only schools, but village halls and even pubs), so there would be a shift system and much more free time than usual.

I think we have *just* what you're looking for...

Don't like the look of him!

One of the most uncomfortable moments in a new evacuee's life was standing in a crowd, with a name-and-address label stuck to your coat, waiting to be chosen by people who were being forced by the government to give up their spare rooms to the incomers.

It was a bit like being an animal paraded at a show – and they didn't always want you.

I'll have this one!

If you had brothers and sisters, you couldn't be sure that you would all be billeted together, and you could only hope that the families who took you in (your new Uncle and Aunty) were kind and decent.

As for the host families, who do you think they would choose to share their home:

- The beautiful blonde girl with the big, blue eyes?
- The tall, strapping lad just made for baling hay on the farm?
- The angry-looking little vixen at the back who's stamping her feet?
- That spotty boy with a finger up his nose?

Country life

It was often a first taste of country living for the evacuated boys and girls, and it must have been a shock for them to exchange rows of houses and busy roads for open fields and muddy lanes.

Those from a comfortable background found it a bit unsettling. You couldn't just jump on a bus or an underground train, but you had to walk everywhere. There was probably no cinema nearby, and very few shops.

Evacuees often had to get used to primitive country toilets – perhaps little more than a bucket in an outhouse. (Of course, some of these kids came from poorer parts of London where outdoor toilets were still common long after the war.) Water might have to be fetched from wells or rivers, and paraffin might be the only fuel for lighting and cooking.

Mind you, many of them loved it – especially if life at home hadn't been very happy and if they had the luck to fall in with new guardians who showed them genuine affection. Then they blossomed.

Indeed, some of them got on so well in their new 'digs' that they made friends for life, and would return to see their host families for many years afterwards.

Some of them came from city slums, and for them it was 'a land of milk and honey' – wonderful fresh air, room to roam and all the food they could eat.

R uby discovers that milk doesn't always come from bottles.

For some of the slum children, sleeping in clean sheets and wearing laundered clothes must have seemed like true luxury.

And some of them became expert at looking after large animals which had terrified them at first – perhaps because they had never set eyes on one before.

Just imagine coming face to face with a cow for the first time, with those trampling hooves and sharp-looking horns! But children soon get used to new things, and many found that they enjoyed mucking in on the farm.

Children like this could be very useful, and looking after livestock became a daily routine. The farmer was paid for having the children, and he had unpaid labour, too!

But some of the 'natives', who were used to a slower pace of life, looked upon these noisy invaders as a strange and rather dangerous breed of animal.

The fact is, as we've noted, that many evacuees came from the poorest areas of

British cities, and these were the kind of rude comments often made about them:

- They were underfed.
- They wore threadbare clothes.
- They had nits. (Who doesn't these days?)
- They weren't used to taking a bath.
- They employed a somewhat spicy use of language.

An elderly, well-to-do couple with a house large enough to take evacuees might well find these young whippersnappers difficult to cope with, especially if they had never had children of their own.

And then there was the bed-wetting. A lot of former evacuees speak about that. Who could blame a lonely, frightened young child for waking up to soaking-wet sheets? Well, many host families did blame them – and were very unsympathetic about it.

In fact, both sides often found it a hard slog. Sometimes host families handed children back to the authorities, despairing of ever being able to cope with their waywardness. And sometimes the children 'did a bunk', escaping from oppressive households and making a brave attempt to find their way home, however far off it was. Some tried to hide out in local woods, living on wild berries and anything they could scrounge.

Nobody at home

But what if there was nobody back home to run to?

Tragically, some evacuee children never saw their parents again because they had been killed by German bombing during the Blitz. That was a bad enough sorrow to bear.

Others, though, were simply abandoned. Their parents never bothered to visit them while they were away, and when the war was over they returned 'home' to find their house flattened or empty and their family nowhere to be seen.

Surely there had been some mistake, and they would soon be reunited? But no: the shocking fact is that nearly 40,000 evacuee children were left unclaimed by their parents.

What happened to these waifs whom nobody seemed to want?

- Some were adopted by the families who had looked after them during the war.
- Some were put into orphanages.
- Some of the older ones disappeared, found work and created new lives for themselves.

It wasn't until six months after the war was over that the evacuee scheme finally came to an end. At that late stage there were still more than 5,000 children living with host families, and some 3,500,000 people in all (most of them children) had experienced the rough-and-tumble of an evacuee's life.

For most, no doubt, it was better than braving the incessant bombing of the Blitz. Yet many of those left behind (parents weren't *forced* to send their children away) found the daily bombardment of their streets rather exciting. Shrapnel-collecting became a brand-new hobby for them...

CHAPTER TWO

BLOWN TO SMITHEREENS

I t was soon clear that something different was happening. On the afternoon of Saturday 7 September 1940, a vast swarm of 348 German bombers flanked by more than 600 Messerschmitt fighters crossed the Channel from northern France – and kept going.

Normally the formation would break up, to attack airfields, oil installations and the like, with British Spitfires and Hurricanes harrying them at every turn. But not this time: the planes droned on all the way to London, and by six in the evening the capital was ablaze.

The planes out to get you

Some Londoners became skilled at recognising not only the shapes but the engine sounds of the planes sent over to attack them. These were the main ones:

- **Messerschmitt Bf 109.** A single-seater fighter mounted with cannon and machine guns. Very fast and used in combat against the Spitfire.

- **Junkers Ju 88.** A medium-sized bomber with the speed of a fighter. Carried a four-man crew and was extremely versatile.

- **Heinkel He 111.** The largest of the bombers that flew over England, with a wing span of 14.3 metres. It had a five-man crew, had two engines and was armed with a cannon, six machine guns and a bomb load of around 10,000 kg.

- **Dornier Do 217.** A latecomer, entering service in 1941, this was a large, twin-engined aircraft used mainly as a night bomber. It had a crew of four and was fitted with machine guns and cannon. Its bomb load was around 9,000 kg.

He 111

Yet the Luftwaffe had even more in store for what was to be known as 'Black Saturday'. At eight o'clock that same evening another 300 bombers came in, and their attack lasted until half past four the following morning.

The army chiefs of staff were convinced that this ferocity signalled the onset of Hitler's invasion of Britain, so they immediately ordered troops to take up their battle stations and blow up bridges to thwart a German advance.

They were wrong. What it signalled was the end of the Battle of Britain and the beginning of the Blitz.

Some Black Saturday statistics:

- 430 people were killed.
- 1,600 were seriously injured.
- Many thousands were left homeless.

Londoners had never known anything like it, but they would very soon come to expect much more of the same: the bombers returned to do their deadly work for 76 of the following 77 nights.

The bombs out to get you

The Germans invented a wide range of dangerous explosives to drop from the skies:

- **Incendiary devices (or firebombs).** These would start raging fires at very high temperatures.

- **High-explosive bombs.** They came in various shapes and sizes, and just one of them could flatten several houses.

- **Landmines** (see page 9). These metal canisters, shaped like a large dustbin, were dropped by parachute and were intended to explode on landing.

- **V-1s (or buzz bombs, or doodlebugs).** These long, cross-shaped, jet-powered flying bombs (illustrated on page 60) were introduced in 1944. They had just enough fuel to reach London – and when their buzzing engines cut out you waited for the big bang.

- **V-2s.** Deadly ballistic missiles propelled into London faster than the speed of sound from September 1944 onwards. The scariest of the lot, because you couldn't hear it coming.

- **UXBs.** Unexploded bombs. Nobody knows how many of these are still there.

I don't care which of you is Mr Churchill – get down here at once.

London Blitz statistics

7 September 1940 – 11 May 1941

- 40,000 civilians killed
- 46,000 seriously injured
- 150 raids in 200 days
- 18,000 tonnes of high explosive dropped
- 1,000,000 homes destroyed or badly damaged
- 40% of houses in Stepney destroyed

And it could have been even worse!

The government forecast (but of course didn't tell anyone) that during the first six months of the war there would be:

- 600,000 civilians killed
- 1,200,000 injured

So they:

- stockpiled thousands of cardboard coffins
- printed a million burial forms.

Thank goodness they were wrong!

By mid-November 13,000 tonnes of high explosives and a million incendiary bombs had been dropped on London – and only one in a hundred of the German planes had been shot down.

One's house is hit

The first areas to suffer were the docklands by the Thames and the 'Cockney' territory of the East End. These were the poorest parts of the city – which seemed pretty unfair, to say the least.

Later, though, some of the famous buildings in the West End were targeted, including Westminster Abbey, the House of Commons and Buckingham Palace (three times).

King George VI and Queen Elizabeth had decided to stay in the capital, rather than retreat to the safety of one of their country houses. This won them the affection of ordinary Londoners, and the Queen took some comfort from the (minor) damage to her palace, saying that she could now 'look the East End in the face'.

Taking advantage

Many stories about people 'all pulling together' in wartime are absolutely true, but there were also plenty of rogues about who took advantage of the Blitz and its victims.

Bombed houses were easy prey to thieves, and in the first two months of the Blitz alone nearly 400 cases were brought to the courts. Some of the culprits were the very people whose job it was to help, such as firefighters and policemen.

The Mayor of London was so angry that he said people should be reminded that they could be hanged for the offence. (The courts were rather more lenient than that.)

And then there were the people who pretended to have been 'bombed out' so that they could claim large amounts of compensation from the government.

One man was imprisoned for three years when it turned out that he'd claimed to have been made homeless 19 times in just five months.

A bomb at the palace

On the morning of 13 September 1940, the Germans almost achieved what would have been a mighty propaganda triumph – the killing of the King and Queen of England.

The Queen described what happened in a letter to her mother-in-law later that day. She was on one of the upper floors at Buckingham Palace helping the King get an eyelash out of his eye when they heard an aircraft diving down towards them and the scream of a bomb.

'It all happened so quickly,' she wrote, 'that we had only time to look foolishly at each other when the scream hurtled past us and exploded with a tremendous crash in the quadrangle.

'I saw a great column of smoke and earth thrown up into the air, and then we all ducked like lightning into the corridor.'

Her letter ended: 'P.S. Dear old B.P. is still standing and that is the main thing.'

'Ang on a mo'!

Unfortunately London's defences weren't up to the job of keeping the Luftwaffe out.

One smart idea was to create what looked like herds of aerial elephants. Huge 'barrage balloons', filled with lighter-than-air gas and anchored to the ground by steel cables, kept out low-flying aircraft. But:

- Few of the British fighter aircraft could operate at night, when most raids took place.
- The searchlights which were supposed to pick out the incoming bombers so they could be shot down were underpowered.
- British anti-aircraft ('ack-ack') guns were primitive, and there were only 92 of them available on the first night of the Blitz.

By the end of September (in just 24 days) 5,730 people had been killed and nearly 10,000 badly injured. Hospitals, some of them damaged, were full to overflowing.

Barrage balloon

The deadliest bomb

On the night of 10 September 1940, large numbers of East End families bombed out of their houses in West Ham were sheltering in Hallsville Road school while waiting for transport that would take them away to safety. The transport never came, and a German bomb flattened the building. The council's official death toll was 73, but local people believed that the true figure was nearer 400.

St Paul's survives

Ever wondered why St Paul's Cathedral has so little stained glass? It was all blown out during a wartime raid. (The only stained glass now is in the memorial chapel to fallen American soldiers.) The cathedral's architect, Sir Christopher Wren, would have been quite happy to see today's plain glass, though – because that's what he'd intended in the first place!

Although the bombing caused minor damage to the area around the high altar, the cathedral somehow survived the relentless night-time attacks all around it, the great dome standing out defiantly against a smoke-filled sky.

47

Ten hit songs of the war

1. **Accentuate the Positive** Johnny Mercer
2. **Boogie-Woogie Bugle Boy** Andrews Sisters
3. **Idaho** Benny Goodman Orchestra
4. **I'm Making Believe** The Inkspots
5. **Sentimental Journey** Les Brown Orchestra
6. **Sunrise Serenade** Glenn Miller Orchestra
7. **Take the 'A' Train** Duke Ellington Orchestra
8. **We'll Meet Again** Vera Lynn
9. **White Christmas** Bing Crosby
10. **Yours** Jimmy Dorsey Orchestra

The very worst night

Saturday 10 May 1941 marks the end of the Blitz 'proper', because after that Hitler turned his attentions to the Russian front and (until the V-1s and V-2s arrived), London and other British cities were less severely assaulted.

But – as in the best-run firework displays – the biggest bang was saved for last. On this night 500 Luftwaffe planes dropped a massive 700 tonnes of explosive on London in a relentless barrage. For those who took the brunt of it, the night seemed as if it would never end.

Thousands of fires raged through the buildings and streets, with whole areas devastated.

- **1,500 people were killed.**
- **1,800 were seriously injured.**
- **11,000 homes were damaged.**

This was the night on which the House of Commons took a hit, but so too did countless other public buildings, including Waterloo Station and the British Museum.

The Queen's Hall in Langham Place, across the road from the BBC's headquarters, was virtually destroyed by an incendiary – only hours after 2,400 people had filled it to hear an orchestral concert conducted by the famous Sir Malcolm Sargent.

So vast was the damage that twenty years later London would still bear the scars, with flattened, weed-filled bomb-sites not yet redeveloped.

How on earth did people put up with it?

CHAPTER THREE

TAKING PRECAUTIONS

The way that some people go on about it, you'd think that Hitler was defeated by the British sense of humour. The truth is that the ability to see the funny side of Blitz life must have been a godsend. After all, there was precious little you could do during the dreadful nightly bombings except take the obvious precautions and try to keep your spirits up.

And, let's face it, how could you take anyone seriously if you saw them coming towards you wearing a weird gas mask that made them look like Mickey Mouse?

Anderson shelter

Earth

Corrugated steel

Well, the house is still
there, Bert, but
where's Tibbles?

Gruesome gas masks

In the end, no-one needed a gas mask because the Germans didn't use chemical weapons in Britain. But they *had* used deadly mustard gas in the trenches during the First World War. That's why the government thought it best to hand out 38 million masks just in case.

Some facts about gas masks:

- They were made of smelly rubber, got sweaty inside and made some people feel horribly sick.
- Adults had boring black ones, but children's masks were red and blue.
- There were babies' gas helmets, into which mothers would pump air with bellows.

Child's gas mask

Baby respirator

The two things you always had to carry with you were your identity card (in case something nasty happened to you) and your gas mask – although not everybody did.

Children would be given practice lessons at school to make sure they knew how to strap them on.

They weren't taught how to make rude noises by blowing into the flap at the front, but they seemed to pick this up very quickly by themselves.

Outside in the streets, air-raid wardens carried rattles – just like the ones fans used to make a din with at football matches in the old days. They were supposed to swing these about their heads in the event of a gas attack. They also had a whistle to let you know that it was safe to take your mask off.

There were 'gas detectors' on street corners, which would – or so people hoped – light up if there was any gas in the air, and the tops of Post Office pillar boxes were given a coat of gas-detector paint.

Taking shelter

Although gas masks were, as it turned out, an unnecessary precaution, air-raid shelters (or bomb shelters) were used by millions and saved countless lives. There were various kinds:

• Communal shelters
Public shelters made of brick nearly 5 metres thick with reinforced concrete roofs were put up by the government. These would house about 50 people and were fitted with bunks, but they couldn't cope with the large numbers who wanted to use them.

• Underground stations
Of course these weren't really meant to be shelters at all, and at the beginning of the war they were locked so that people couldn't use them.

This caused such an outcry (sometimes the doors were forced open so that everyone could pour in) that the government finally relented – and at one time there were an estimated 177,000 people occupying 79 tube stations every night.

As you can imagine, this wasn't a very pleasant experience, because at first there were no lavatories (you brought your own necessities), and even later, when some basic facilities were provided, the air wasn't sweet-smelling with all those bodies cooped up for the night.

Bethnal Green tube disaster

The air-raid sirens sounded on the evening of 3 March 1943, and hundreds of people began a rapid descent into Bethnal Green underground station on the Central Line.

When a new kind of anti-aircraft rocket was fired a short distance away, the loud and unfamiliar explosion produced a general panic.

A woman, perhaps carrying a baby, tripped on the stairs. The lighting was poor and there were no safety barriers. Other people tumbled on top of her, and within a few seconds 300 people were pressed tight in the tiny stairwell.

As many as 173 people were crushed to death, including more than 60 children.

Eventually bunk beds were installed in the underground stations, and some people found the experience quite cosy. Women would come along the platform with boxes strung around their necks like ice-cream sellers in cinemas, and they would have things like sandwiches, Lyons' fruit pies and bread pudding for sale.

They would also have vast amounts of tea, because in those days Londoners drank hardly any coffee, even when it was available – and it was in short supply during the war.

But even underground you weren't always safe. There were three direct hits on tube stations:

- On 16 September 1940, twenty people were killed at Marble Arch.
- On 14 October 1940, a bomb went through the road and tunnel at Balham tube station, blew up the water mains and sewage pipes, and killed 68 people who were trapped inside.
- On 11 January 1941, the road above Bank station collapsed and 56 people were killed.

• Morrison shelters

Named after the home secretary, Herbert Morrison, these were, in effect, steel cages in your own home, with room for two or three people. You lifted up one of the mesh sides and crawled in – just like your pet hamster.

Some people preferred to snuggle up in under-stair cupboards or go down to their basements. A few believed in fate and felt that if a bomb 'had your name on it' there wasn't much point in trying to hide from it at all.

• Anderson shelters

These corrugated-iron structures (see page 52) were the back-garden alternative. They were named after Sir John Anderson, who was in charge of air-raid precautions. By September 1939 nearly one and a half million of them had been delivered.

The snag for the less energetic was that you had to dig a big hole for them, because they were half-buried in the ground. The snag for the non-handyman was that you had to put them together yourself – unless you could fnd some Boy Scouts to do it for you.

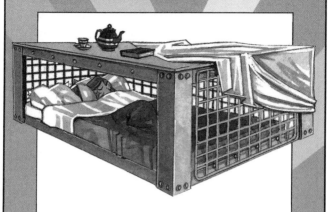

The Morrison shelter was designed to protect its occupants from falling debris if the house was damaged by a bomb.

Survive the Blitz in the comfort of your own home!

Designed to accommodate six people, Anderson shelters were made from curved sheets bolted together at the top, with steel plates at either end, and the entrance was protected by a steel shield and an earthen blast wall.

Whether you fitted a door and put in proper flooring was up to you – as was everything else. The result could be a rather cramped home-from-home (larger people found it difficult to squeeze through the door) or a seedy little dungeon.

V-1 rocket ('doodlebug')

Invading the Savoy

To highlight the plight of the people of Stepney in the East End of London, the local Communist councillor Phil Piratin led a group of 50 people, including some 'ill-clad children', into the glitzy Savoy Hotel in the Strand.

With the help of some sympathetic waiters they occupied the hotel's air-raid shelter, saying that if it was good enough for the rich it was good enough for working-class Stepney families.

At this moment the air-raid sirens sounded. The hotel manager realised that he couldn't very well send the 'invaders' outside into danger – and soon the catering staff came in carrying silver trays laden with pots of tea, bread and butter for the children.

A sheltered upbringing

At least one baby is said to have been born in an Anderson shelter. It was usual in those days for children to be born at home rather than in hospital – and if your home had been damaged, the shelter might be the safest place for the new mother to give birth!

Most people remember the shelters as being very cold and damp. It was a good idea to dig a deeper hole, called a sump, in the floor so that the water could gather in it. Then you'd bail it out with a jug or a saucepan.

Once tucked in for the night, you could play cards or board games, read by torchlight and listen to the radio – although in a particularly heavy bombing raid it would be difficult to hear it above the racket.

And then, when you came out of your hidey-hole, you had to get used to the new world around you.

New? Well, the chances were that a lot of the buildings you knew had been flattened and moved around since you last looked.

And to add to the confusion, everything was pitch-black...

CHAPTER FOUR

THE BLACKOUT
AND OTHER NUISANCES

Preventing the slightest glimmer of light from emerging into the night sky became a Blitz obsession – though the tiny glow from a cigarette surely couldn't have been all that useful to a German pilot flying high above the barrage balloons.

But the authorities were taking no chances. You'd be reported, and possibly fined, if you were caught breaking the rules. Even a man who lit a match in the street to find his false teeth was taken to court. (Did he gnash them with frustration?)

If anyone showed a light, air-raid wardens were expected to show zero tolerance.

Windows were already covered with sticky tape to prevent the glass shattering. Now they had to be completely obscured, and cheap cotton cloth was provided for those who couldn't afford anything better. Householders would spend hours tacking the stuff up, or putting cardboard against the glass, only to find that there were still chinks of light visible in the cracks that had been missed. Oops!

And then you'd have to take it down in the daytime (or live like a cave-dweller) and go through all the hanging-up business again the following evening.

Shops had to obey the same rules, and their owners were expected to devise a way of allowing customers to come in and out without any light sneaking into the street.

Of course all this caused problems, unless you were a bat:

• Street lights were either switched off altogether or dimmed and shielded, and you could use a torch only if the beam was masked.

Wartime entertainment

When you needed to take your mind off nasty things like bombs and a possible invasion, there were plenty of options.

• Radio
Only 20,000 people had television sets, and the service was closed down during the war in any case, but the BBC's 'wireless' programmes were ideal for families during the blackout.

Comedians such as Arthur Askey and Tommy Handley (whose programme *ITMA* stood for *It's That Man Again*) sound pretty UNfunny today, but they did a great job of raising spirits in a dark time. Their catch-phrases, such as 'TTFN' ('Ta-ta for now!') could be heard on every bus and street corner.

Newsreaders such as John Snagge and Alvar Lidell gave listeners the latest war news (somewhat censored, of course), and Prime Minister Winston Churchill's stirring speeches were heard over the airwaves.

• Cinema
People braved the Blitz in droves to see the latest films, which offered a romantic escape from reality.

At the beginning of the war the government had closed the cinemas down, but it soon realised

their value in lifting morale and spreading the official 'message' through propaganda films and Pathé news bulletins.

• Dancing
Millions danced the evenings away to the latest 'swing' tunes played by big bands. And many a romance began in the dance halls, too – some with American and Canadian soldiers.

• Concert parties
ENSA (Entertainments National Service Association) travelled widely to put on concerts, revues and plays both for the armed forces and for civilians.

Some lampposts and tree trunks were painted white to give you just a tiny bit of help.

As you stumbled along you were likely to crack your head or your shins on immoveable objects, and one government poster read: 'Wait! Count 15 slowly before moving in the blackout.'

• Traffic lights and vehicle headlights were fitted with slotted cones, which made them much harder to see. As you'd guess, this led to a sharp increase in the number of accidents, even though the speed limit was reduced to 20 mph (32 kph). The king's surgeon, Wilfred Potter – who thought the blackout was a sign of panic – wrote that the Luftwaffe was able to kill 600 British citizens a month without ever taking to the air. (This figure, mercifully, was an exaggeration.)

Bright ideas for showing motorists that you existed included carrying a white handkerchief – presumably stretching it out in front of you – and (if you were a man) walking along with your shirt tails hanging out of the back of your trousers. Daft!

*a song from the 1920s that was still popular at this time

The Blackout Ripper

This is a nasty murder story, so skip it if you're feeling squeamish.

During February 1942 four young women were violently killed in the West End of London. People were reminded of Jack the Ripper in Victorian times. Women on their own were scared to go out on the streets during the blackout.

The killer might well have continued to terrorise the area for a long time, had a delivery boy not interrupted him just as he was about to commit a fifth murder.

While making his escape, the man dropped his gas mask. These were all numbered (his was no. 525987), which gave the police the easy task of picking up its owner, 27-year-old Gordon Cummins.

It turned out that he was an officer cadet in the RAF, training to fly Spitfires.

He was hanged at Wandsworth Prison that June – during an air raid.

• Buses and trains were fitted with blinds, and their interior lights were extinguished during bombing raids. The bulbs inside trains were painted blue for good measure.

So when your train came to a halt, you had to guess whether it had arrived at its destination or was simply waiting for a signal. You opened the door, and found that you were indeed at a station – but which one? All the signs had been taken down so that invading Germans wouldn't know where they were!

As for passengers arriving at a station, they would find the place in complete darkness, which made it all too easy to take a step too far and plunge from the platform onto the rails. This happened.

Mind you, Underground trains did give out flashes of light from their rails, and passengers would cross their fingers when their carriages came out of the tunnel into an open-air section. They were told that German pilots looked out for that kind of thing – and there was nothing they could do about it.

These measures would undoubtedly have confused Hitler's army had it invaded, but in the meantime they confused a lot of the inhabitants instead!

One poor man out in the countryside took a wrong turning and followed a track leading down to the canal. He fell in and drowned before anyone could answer his cries for help.

An ambulance driver, attempting to take patients from London to a hospital in Essex, got completely lost and found himself driving over a ploughed field. To his embarrassment

The unhealthy blackout

Closing up windows and cracks in door frames inevitably had an effect on ventilation in the home. This caused an increase in coughs and throat infections.

the wounded passengers had to be stretchered to safety through a hedge.

And a nervous young man on his way home from a country pub was suddenly aware of a huge thing coming at him in the darkness. He was terrified – but fortunately it was only a runaway horse!

Where am I?

As if the darkness wasn't enough, travelling was made difficult, especially in country areas, by the removal of road signs. Shop fascia boards were also taken down or changed, to remove the names of towns and villages from them: 'The —————— Stores'.

In fact, for anyone living alongside a likely invasion route the world looked a very different place during the war years.

Down at the coast, the beaches were mined and littered with tank traps and coils of barbed wire. Seaside piers had their central planking taken out so that the enemy couldn't use them as landing stages.

Bamboozling the enemy

Plunging cities into darkness wasn't the only way of foxing enemy pilots. The government came up with some ingenious methods of camouflaging important sites.

- Airfield buildings would be painted green, yellow and brown and decorated to look like fields with trees and ploughed furrows. The grassed runways themselves were painted to look like very small fields with hedges – with no possible room for a plane to land.

- Pill boxes (small concrete fortifications erected at road junctions and along rivers and canals) were disguised as tea rooms, public lavatories, petrol stations and haystacks.

- Coastal gun batteries were transformed into holiday-camp chalets.

- Munitions factories, making bullets and explosives, were made to look like duck ponds.

The paintbrush had become a war weapon!

Inland, obstructions of various kinds, from concrete blocks to old cars and tractors, were set down at strategic points to slow down a German advance.

All along the river and canal approaches sturdy concrete 'pill boxes' were built, so that brave, last-ditch defenders could take pot-shots at the enemy.

Some of them were so sturdy, in fact, that they're still in place to this very day, because it would take so much effort to blow them up. Can you find any near you?

And if the invaders got past that lot? Why, then they'd have to face a noble breed of men – and women – who were being trained to put yet another spanner in their works...

If those Germans ever made it to Dorking, Reg Perkins would be waiting for them.

CHAPTER five

THE PEOPLE'S WAR

Anthony Eden, Secretary of State for War, could hardly believe it. On a May evening in 1940 he'd given a speech on the wireless calling for men who were too old or too young for the army to join a new local defence corps. Within 24 hours a staggering quarter of a million men had signed up, and by the end of July the figure was well over a million.

At first they were the Local Defence Volunteers (LDV), but Churchill changed the name to the more important-sounding Home Guard. These days we like to call them 'Dad's Army'.

Who had to enlist?

In October 1939 every able-bodied man aged between 18 and 41 was told to be ready to serve in the army, navy or air force.

At first only men between the ages of 20 and 23 were conscripted (forced to join up), but the net spread wider as the war continued and in June 1941 40-year-olds received their call-up papers.

In that year single women aged between 20 and 30 were also drafted, but not in order to fight: they were given work in factories, on farms and in offices.

Who could stay behind?

Those in 'reserved occupations' – jobs that were considered essential at home – were not called up. They included:

• dock workers
• farmers
• merchant seamen
• miners
• railway workers
• scientists
• workers in the utility industries: electricity, gas and water.

If you've seen the 1970s sitcom of that name, you'll realise that the idea of these raggle-taggle bands of amateurs defending Britain if the Germans invaded was regarded by many as a bit of a joke. Some quipped that LDV stood for 'Look, Duck and Vanish'!

And they certainly didn't have a good start. They were promised uniforms, but at first each man had to make do with only a cap and an armband.

As for weapons, these also took some time to arrive, so the recruits did their evening drill (most were busy working during the daytime) using substitutes such as:

- broom handles
- golf clubs
- truncheons
- pickaxes
- walking sticks.

The public were urged to hand in their spare pistols and shotguns, and 20,000 were given to the Home Guard within just a few months. Some members of the new force were also quite handy at making home-made grenades or 'Molotov cocktails' – beer or fizzy-drink bottles full of petrol, with a simple fuse.

The new units – composed as they were of a motley mixture of farmers, teachers, bank clerks, shopkeepers and so on, many with no military background whatsoever – had the reputation of being independent and somewhat quirky.

They could also be imaginative. The Blackburn battalion formed a homing-pigeon corps. A bird returning to the loft triggered an electric bell in the orderly room, so that a message would be picked up within seconds.

And in nearby Burnley a machine gun was mounted on the top of a steel-plated Rolls Royce hearse, with flaps through which rifles could be fired at the enemy. Unfortunately the wheels collapsed under the weight of this armoured monster, and a new and stronger set had to be found to replace them.

Men suddenly put in charge of Home Guard units sometimes found it hard to adjust to their new responsibilities. One who spent his

B lackburn Home Guard's early-warning system gets airborne.

working life looking after horses on a farm forgot himself while marching his recruits round the streets of the local town. They would have obeyed instantly if he had yelled 'Halt!' when he wanted them to stop in their tracks – but they were confused (and mightily amused) when he barked out 'Whoa!'

It wasn't until 1943 that the War Office finally allowed women to join the Home Guard on a non-combatant basis – giving them the odd title of 'nominated women' and a *plastic* brooch badge with the letters HG encircled by a wreath.

One military officer wrote to the press explaining their duties: they could 'degrease rifles and clean small arms, but not fire them; look after uniforms, but not wear them; and cook rations, but not eat them'.

What the initials stood for

- **AFS** Auxiliary Fire Service
- **ARP** Air Raid Precautions
- **LDV** Local Defence Volunteers (later Home Guard)

He was lucky not to have been hit over the head with one of those broom handles!

In time the Home Guard were provided with proper uniforms and hundreds of thousands of rifles and Sten guns (small machine guns) plus a variety of other weapons, some of them shipped over from the United States.

If the Germans had, indeed, invaded, these units would have slowed down their advance – and in the meantime they had a lot of important jobs to do, including:

- manning aircraft batteries
- patrolling sensitive areas, such as factories, airfields, railway stations and the seafront
- releasing trapped civilians after air raids
- laying anti-tank obstacles
- bomb disposal
- arresting German airmen who had bailed out of their planes.

It was certainly no laughing matter that 1,206 members of the Home Guard lost their lives during the war, with another 557 being seriously injured.

ARP wardens

Churchill called it 'The People's War' for the very good reason that soldiering abroad was only a small part of the overall effort involved in defeating the enemy.

Like members of the Home Guard, the air-raid wardens were civilians (women as well as men) who usually did daytime jobs before turning out for their ARP duties – most of the bombing, of course, coming at night.

Wearing a steel helmet and blue overalls, and armed with a whistle and a bell, they patrolled the streets ready to report any incidents to their Civil Defence control centre. Their tasks included:

- arranging the sounding of the sirens before and after air raids
- evacuating buildings, closing streets and alerting the authorities when there were unexploded bombs
- summoning fire engines, stretcher parties, mobile canteens and other services to areas where bombs had fallen.

They weren't universally popular, because another part of their job was checking that people were carrying their gas masks and making sure that they observed the blackout.

After all, having someone shout 'Put that light out!' in your ear wouldn't particularly endear them to you, would it? The nickname for bossy people like that was 'Little Hitlers'.

But they were everywhere (there were about 1,400,000 of them in all) and they did invaluable work in the darkest days of the Blitz.

Sounding the siren

Messenger boys

Most children left school at 14 in those days, and boys of that age and above were given bicycles and used as messengers. Older teenagers were provided with motorbikes.

They ran errands for all the different wartime services. Fire Guard messengers, for example, wheeled their way through smoke-filled streets to ferry information between ARPs and units detailed to put out fires.

Their toughest job emotionally was delivering telegrams which reported that a family member had been killed on active service or was 'missing in action'.

Other youngsters were involved in training exercises, which could be exciting although sometimes a little dangerous. One lad, whose father was an instructor in the ARP, found himself strapped to a stretcher and lowered to the ground from his granny's first-floor window to help volunteers learn how to rescue people from bombed houses. The window was tiny and the descent was hair-raising.

The Auxiliary fire Service

Here's another vital service that was carried out by part-time men and women. At first they were issued with simple stirrup pumps to squirt water on fires when cities were ablaze.

They also supported the local professional brigades. One rather serious problem for them, though, was that the hydrant valves they used didn't come in standard sizes – so one brigade's hoses couldn't be fitted to the water supply of another's. Not a good idea!

The government at last got its act together, and in 1941 it decided to merge the AFS with the full-timers in a new National Fire Service.

'forced labour'

It's said that for every soldier who fires a gun at the enemy you need something like 50 more behind the battle lines – the people who supply, feed and organise them.

But during the rigours of the Second World War it was obvious that the whole population had to be 'mobilised' in one way or another.

Britain's Minister of Labour and National Service, Ernest Bevin, wasn't keen on forcing people into jobs, but he soon realised that he had no option (see page 90).

Not only were more men and women needed at the front, but another 1,500,000 workers were needed to work in the munitions industries in addition to the 3,500,000 already working there.

And since it was unthinkable that anyone could leave such a job without a very good reason, Bevin introduced legislation called an Essential Work Order, which stipulated that nobody could resign or be sacked from companies in a range of industries:

- engineering
- aircraft manufacture
- shipbuilding
- railways
- coal mining.

Bletchley Park and Enigma

Who won the war for Britain and the Allies? There's no one answer, of course, but the cryptanalysts (codebreakers) who worked at the large house called Bletchley Park in rural Buckinghamshire (it's now open to the public) must feature high on the list.

When the German government and military sent messages to one another they used cypher machines to scramble them into strings of nonsense words so that the British wouldn't be able to read them. The most famous of these machines was called Enigma.

Of course, the Germans had the codes which enabled them to put the words back together again, and they were sure that the British would never be able to 'crack' them. But that's just what a large team of brilliant scientists and puzzle-solvers managed to do at Bletchley Park.

Their amazing feat enabled Winston Churchill and his fellow war leaders to read secret messages sent between enemy commanders and their headquarters, and it played a major part in the destruction of enemy U-boats in the Battle of the Atlantic. Indeed, some say that it shortened the war by two years.

Churchill later described these brilliant intellects as 'my geese that laid the golden eggs and never cackled'.

The Bevin Boys

How would you like to work down a coal mine? More to the point, how would you like to be FORCED to work down a coal mine?

When war broke out there was a shortage of coal to fuel Britain's war industries, and in 1943 the Minister of Labour, Ernest Bevin, decided that he would have to conscript young men of 25 and under who had not yet enlisted in the armed services.

He arranged this through a kind of lottery. One of his secretaries allegedly plucked a number from a hat each week, and all the eligible men who had that digit at the end of their National Service number were added to the list.

This was not a popular idea, and 40 per cent of those whose name came up objected to it. A few hundred had their appeals allowed, 147 went to prison and eventually 21,800 served as 'Bevin Boys' alongside 16,000 other young men who had opted for coal mining when they were called up.

Famous Bevin Boys include the comedian Eric Morecambe (of Morecambe and Wise), the Welsh international footballer Alf Sherwood, the dramatist Peter Shaffer and the DJ and charity worker Sir Jimmy Savile, who later said, 'I went down as a boy and came up as a man.'

On the move

As for those in the so-called 'reserved occupations' (see page 78), they had to be prepared to move around the country if that's what the government needed. When the London docks were badly damaged in the Blitz, for example, it was decided to divert ships to ports such as those on the River Clyde in Scotland instead. That meant some workers were expected to uproot themselves – for the good of their country.

Strike action

Despite the general desire to 'muck in' to help the war effort, many workers were dissatisfied with their pay and conditions.

There were strikes throughout the war, and in 1944 stoppages caused the lost of around 3,700,000 days' production.

The government (supported by the main trades union organisation, the TUC) responded by bringing in Defence Regulation 1AA, which made incitement to strike unlawful.

The George Cross

At the height of the Blitz, impressed by great acts of bravery by ordinary men and women, King George VI decided to create a new medal for civilian non-combatants.

One of the youngest recipients of the George Cross – athough he didn't survive to know it – was 19-year-old Donald Clarke, an apprentice on the tanker *San Emiliano*, set ablaze and sunk in the Battle of the Atlantic. Young Donald died of his injuries after bravely helping to row a lifeboat to safety. His citation read: 'His hands had to be cut away from the oar as the burnt flesh had stuck to it. He had pulled as well as anyone, although he was rowing with the bones of his hands.'

The king declared that the new award was to be equal in importance to the coveted Victoria Cross, which had long been awarded to military personnel for outstanding bravery.

It was, if you like, the People's Cross.

Women in wartime

In December 1941 single women and childless widows between the ages of 20 and 30 were conscripted by the government. They could join one of the women's services – the ATS, the WAAF or the WRNS (see page 94) – or be sent to work in factories.

In addition, all women under 50 – unless they were pregnant, had a young child at home or were caring for an elderly father – had to register at their local labour exchange and could be directed into war work.

By the time the war ended there were 460,000 women in the armed forces and more than six million engaged in civilian war jobs. They were paid less than their male colleagues – and men who came back from service overseas were able to reclaim the jobs they'd had before they left.

• Women's Voluntary Service
These volunteers – well over a million of them – did everything from escorting evacuees to helping refugees, mending soldiers' socks,

lending out wedding dresses, running mobile canteens and delivering goods to the houses of women who were too busy working in factories to shop for themselves.

• **Secret agents**

At the other end of the scale were the brave women of the Special Operations Executive (SOE) who were smuggled into occupied France to help organise the Allied landings in Normandy on D-Day, 6 June 1944. The most famous of them, Violette Szabo and 'Odette', were captured and tortured, and Szabo was murdered by the Gestapo, the cruel German security police. Both were awarded the George Cross.

What the initials stood for

- **ATS** Auxiliary Territorial Service (Army)
- **WAAF** Women's Auxiliary Air Force
- **WLA** Women's Land Army (see p. 144)
- **WRNS** ('Wrens') Women's Royal Naval Service
- **WVS** Women's Voluntary Service

Working in a munitions factory

Elsie discovers a talent she didn't know she had.

Ten films about the Second World War

1. **A Bridge Too Far** (Battle of Arnhem)

2. **Battle of Britain** (See pages 19–22)

3. **Casablanca** (Famous romance set in Morocco)

4. **Sink the Bismarck** (The Germans' huge battleship is destroyed by the British Navy)

5. **Stalingrad** (The Eastern Front as experienced by German soldiers)

6. **The Bridge on the River Kwai** (English prisoners of war in Burma)

7. **The Desert Fox** (The battles of German Field Marshal Erwin Rommel, defeated in North Africa)

8. **The Diary of Anne Frank** (See page 12)

9. **The Great Escape** (True story of escape by Allied prisoners of war from Stalag Luft III)

10. **The Longest Day** (Allied invasion of Normandy on D-Day)

Chapter Six

ADVICE AND PROPAGANDA

Building public morale (that is, making people feel more cheerful and upbeat about things) was a major objective of the Ministry of Information during the war – and its campaign didn't start too brightly.

The government produced a series of posters which people felt insulted their intelligence, as if they didn't know how to behave properly without being told.

Some of them also took an awfully long time to read: 'Your Courage, Your Cheerfulness,

Films about heroism helped those at home to feel less helpless about the war.

Muriel felt a lump in her throat as Douglas's Spitfire soared into the air. Would he ever make it back?

Your Resolution Will Bring Us Victory,' for example, and 'Don't Help the Enemy, Careless Talk May Give Away Vital Secrets.' A snappier one, 'Keep Calm and Carry On,' was printed but never used. After all, who needed to be told?

The Times newspaper said these were 'egregious and unnecessary exhortations' (you can look those words up in a dictionary if you like), while the more down-to-earth *Daily Express* spoke more simply of 'waste and paste'.

What is propaganda?

Propaganda is any material – such as writing or films – intended to spread a powerful message and to win over the hearts and minds of the people who receive it.

It's often exaggerated or downright dishonest, which is why it has a bad name. But people defend their own propaganda, because they're sure it's being used in a good cause.

Enter Brendan Bracken

By the middle of 1941 three ministers of information had come and gone, and it was then that Winston Churchill brought in the 40-year-old Brendan Bracken to shake the ministry up.

He wasn't everyone's favourite. To begin with, he was slightly odd-looking. Although tall and well dressed, he had very bad teeth and a shock of unruly red hair. In addition he had the habit of talking in long monologues. He was so full of his own ideas that he didn't let anyone else get a word in edgeways.

No weather!

The British may love talking about the weather, but they had to do without their forecasts during the war years. Any mention of the outlook for the following ten days was banned – in case it might help the Luftwaffe to plan bombing raids.

But Bracken was a successful magazine publisher, and his understanding of how the news industry worked made all the difference.

The ministry's work covered three areas:

- improving public morale
- producing information and advice
- controlling (that is, censoring) what appeared in the media (newspapers and radio).

Bracken, as we shall see, certainly didn't put a stop to posters, slogans and propaganda films, but he thought the best way to motivate those suffering the horrors of the Blitz was to give them as much information as he could.

As for the media, although Bracken had 'emergency powers' to decide which news and other information should appear in the press, on the radio and in films, he promised editors that he would put a gag only on military information and anything else that might be useful to the enemy.

This put those editors on the spot. They had to make difficult decisions about what it would be right to include.

Some wartime slogans

BE LIKE DAD – KEEP MUM
This wouldn't do at all today, but before the war most women gave up work when they married, and were 'kept' by their husbands. 'Keeping mum' also meant staying quiet – in other words, not saying anything that could be useful to an enemy spy.

KEEP MUM – SHE'S NOT SO DUMB
A rather strange version of the above.

CARELESS TALK COSTS LIVES

TITTLE TATTLE LOST THE BATTLE
Two more on the 'hush, hush' theme.

COME ON, WOMEN, MAN THE FACTORIES
A little confusion here, surely! But women played a vital role in making munitions.

COUGHS AND SNEEZES SPREAD DISEASES
In other words, 'Please use a handkerchief.' It may seem odd for the government to bother with this kind of advice, but it needed everyone fit and well in order to pursue the war effort.

MAKE DO AND MEND
With clothing and other materials in short supply, people were encouraged to repair what they already had rather than go out and buy replacements.

DIG FOR VICTORY
Food was scarce, too, so the answer was to grow your own (see Chapter 8).

YOUR BRITAIN – FIGHT FOR IT NOW
This one appeared on recruiting posters, some of them featuring romantic paintings of the peaceful British countryside.

There was a great debate in one newsroom about whether to reveal that there was to be a football match involving workers from Battersea Power Station. Suppose the Germans found out that we had a power station there!

(Of course they knew this very well. They had detailed maps of London and all the other areas they wanted to attack.)

flying nuns!

Rumours always spread in wartime. One which went the rounds in Britain was that there was a unit of German soldiers dressed as nuns about to be dropped into the countryside. It would have been great fun to see!

Billy Brown

One character who became famous during the war years was Billy Brown of London Town, a cartoon character dressed as a City 'gent' with pin-striped trousers, a bowler hat and an umbrella. He was created by the cartoonist David Langdon.

Billy gave the public the government's advice in verse about how to behave in various situations – in the blackout, in queues, on public transport and so on.

He may have been infuriatingly smug, but he at least brought out the British public's sense of humour. One of his ditties, aimed at preventing congestion near bus doors, ran:

> *Kindly pass along the bus*
> *And so make room for all of us.*

Below this someone scrawled:

> *That's all right without a doubt,*
> *But how the heck do we get out?*

Some writers and artists who worked for the Ministry

• **John Betjeman**
He later became the poet laureate, but during the war he worked for the Ministry's film unit.

• **Kenneth Bird**
The art editor of the humorous magazine *Punch*, who signed his work as Fougasse, designed several witty cartoons on the 'Careless Talk Costs Lives' theme. A famous one shows an enormous German general and his sidekick sitting behind two gossiping women on the bus.

• **Alfred Hitchcock**
The famous director of suspense films made two French-language propaganda films, *Aventure malgache (Madagascan Adventure)* and *Bon Voyage*. They were good films but they weren't considered to be effective propaganda – so they were never shown.

• **Henry Moore**
The noted sculptor was one of Britain's official war artists. Their job was to paint not only war scenes, but things like people at work and sheltering in underground stations.

• **Paul Nash**
Regarded by many as the greatest British artist of the 20th century, he had the distinction of

being an official war artist in both world wars. One of his most famous paintings of the Second World War is a landscape littered with wrecked German planes. Of the Blitz he wrote: 'Suddenly the sky was upon us all like a huge hawk hovering, threatening. Everyone was searching the sky expecting some terror to fall.'

• P. L. Travers
You may know her as the author of the Mary Poppins books, but after the Ministry sent her to America she wrote *I Go By Sea, I Go By Land*, which tells the stories of British evacuees and their reactions to the New World.

A war artist at work

Billy also ticked off people who were tempted to peel tape off train windows in the blackout to discover where they were:

I trust you'll pardon my correction,
That stuff is there for your protection.

Perhaps you can think of a two-line reply yourself. This is what one passenger wrote:

Thank you for your information,
But I can't see the bloomin' station!

Someone can't count!

Here's a typical example of how governments use propaganda.

The British said that they had shot down 2,698 German planes during the Battle of Britain. The true number was probably below 1,300.

The Germans said they had shot down 3,058 British planes, but the RAF didn't actually have that many! They really lost fewer than 800.

It was still quite a lot, admittedly.

Artists at war

Brendan Bracken used many of the leading writers, artists and film-makers of the day to produce both straightforward public information and powerful propaganda.

He also created a Ministry of Information film unit, which made as many as 1,887 films during the war. These would be seen not only in cinemas, but in church halls and factories – indeed, wherever people could be enticed to watch them.

Many were 'shorts' which gave advice on such basic things as blood transfusions and garden composting, but others were stirring, full-length dramas.

Fires Were Started, for instance, depicted a thrilling day and night with the National Fire Service during the Blitz, using real firemen, while *Listen to Britain* gave a stirring picture of ordinary Britons getting on with their lives despite the bombing.

Mass Observation

Reading other people's letters and diaries is something most of us find interesting, but to know what people were thinking and feeling during the war was particularly useful for the government.

Fortunately they were given just what they needed by an organisation called Mass Observation, which had been set up in 1937.

Ordinary men and women agreed to send in reports about their lives, however insignificant they might seem to be, and these were stored in an ever-growing archive.

Some of the contributors were suffering the nightly Blitz bombardments, while others were in safer areas away from the bombing. Together they gave a rounded picture of British morale and how the public was coping with shortages and other restrictions.

Mass Observation, based at the University of Sussex, is still collecting reports of people's 'commonplace' lives today.

'One day,' thought Charles, 'this war will be history.'

Ten children's novels about the Second World War

1. **A Candle in the Dark** Adèle Geras

2. **Adolphus Tips** Michael Morpurgo

3. **Blitzcat** Robert Westall

4. **Carrie's War** Nina Bawden

5. **Goodnight, Mister Tom**
   Michelle Magorian

6. **Never Say Goodbye** Hilary Green

7. **Once** Morris Gleitzman

8. **The Boy in the Striped Pyjamas**
   Mark Herman

9. **When Hitler Stole Pink Rabbit**
   Judith Kerr

10. **When the Siren Wailed** Noel Streatfeild

Desert Victory

The harsh truth was that putting up with things – keeping 'a stiff upper lip' – was the best people could hope to do for a very long time.

It wasn't until November 1942 – more than three years into the war – that they could celebrate a first British victory over German forces, when General Montgomery's 8th Army defeated the Afrika Korps at the Battle of El Alamein in the North African desert.

At the outbreak of war there hadn't been a single cameraman in uniform, but thanks largely to Brendan Bracken there was now a large team of them in place to make the powerful film *Desert Victory*. It was shown in 81 countries and dubbed into 15 languages – wonderful propaganda!

It was a crucial moment in the war. As Churchill said later, 'Before Alamein we never had a victory; after Alamein we never had a defeat.'

General Montgomery (known to his troops as Monty) was himself a man who understood the importance of morale.

He knew what sacrifices his men were making in the face of the German guns, and he was almost fanatical about reaching out to every last soldier in the speeches he gave before a battle.

But, as we know, they weren't the only ones finding life tough. Back at home, people were suffering not only heavy bombing but severe shortages of food and materials, too.

Get the Coke Habit!

This was the strange title of one of the short features made by the Ministry's film unit.

No, not Coca Cola, and certainly not the illegal drug cocaine – coke is a smokeless fuel used as a substitute for coal.

CHAPTER SEVEN

THE CUPBOARD WAS BARE

Britain was an isolated place in the dark years of the war. Mainland Europe was occupied by German forces, and one in every four ships sailing across the Atlantic from America was being sunk by German U-boats.

In no time at all people found themselves going without things they had always taken for granted. There were shortages of essentials such as food and clothing, and also of 'life's little luxuries' – tea, cigarettes (smoking was still fashionable in those days) and the matches to light them with.

Of course, people with lots of money could always find what they needed by paying a higher price for it, but that wouldn't be fair at a time when every family was suffering in one way or another.

That's why, in January 1940, the government introduced rationing. It was a way of sharing things equally.

Mind you, having the coupons for something (see opposite) didn't necessarily mean that you could afford it. There were many poor people who simply didn't have enough money to pay for what they were legally entitled to buy.

One week's ration for an adult might look something like this (see page 118).

How rationing worked

Every household had to register with a local shop (you couldn't just buy rationed things anywhere) and there was a ration book for each member of the family.

This had your coupons in it. They weren't a substitute for money. You still had to pay – the coupons were just to tell you how much you were allowed to buy.

How much of each kind of food everyone was allowed depended on how scarce it was at the time – so the cheese quota, for instance, might vary from one month to the next.

With meat you had a little more choice. It was rationed by cost, rather than weight – so you could choose between a small cut of something expensive or a joint of something cheap.

In addition there was a points system. Everyone had the same number of points for items such as canned food. As with meat, you could use all your points on something expensive or spread them over a number of cheaper items.

What was rationed...

As we've seen, the amount you were able to get with your coupons varied at different times, but here are some typical weekly rations for one person:

- bacon and ham: 4 oz (115 g)
- butter: 4 oz (115 g)
- sugar: 12 oz (340 g)
- cheese: 1–8 oz (28–225 g)
- chocolate: 12 oz (340 g)
- milk: 3 pints (1.7 l)

Eggs were 'allocated', not rationed, because their supply varied throughout the year – but everyone was supposed to get an average of just under one a week.

...and what wasn't

Some things were never rationed during the war, including:

- bread (though people didn't like what was called the National Loaf, made of wholemeal)
- vegetables (but they were in short supply)
- fruit (the same, but more so).

There were a few exeptions to the rules:

- Pregnant women and breast-feeding mothers were allowed extra milk and vitamins.
- Children under 5 were entitled to 7 pints (4 litres) of free or subsidised milk a week.
- After 1942 children were also given free orange juice (a nasty-tasting condensed sort) and cod-liver oil – so thank your lucky stars that they're not being dished out to you today.

Lord Woolton's recipes

The Minister for Food, Lord Woolton, who had once been a social worker in Liverpool (his adopted city), was determined that the health of the nation shouldn't suffer just because food was scarce.

Amazingly, he pulled it off. At the end of the war the population was in many ways a lot healthier than it is now.

Perhaps we should all start eating powdered eggs (ugh!) and spam[1] fritters...

---

1. *Spam was a canned meat from America.*

There you go: 12 ounces.

Collecting the sugar ration is one of the highlights of Ruby's week.

The black market

Whenever governments put restrictions on things, there are always 'smart' people who will make money by breaking the rules.

The illegal trade in food covered by rationing was called the 'black market'. Farmers and smallholders would sell their produce to anyone prepared to pay extra for it – and this meant, of course, that there was less to go round for everybody else.

The Ministry of Food employed no fewer than 900 inspectors to deal with the problem, and Parliament passed a law imposing heavy fines and imprisonment on the offenders.

Some shopkeepers were black-marketeers, too. They sold food 'under the counter' – in other words, without anyone knowing – when it should have gone to people with the right coupons in their ration books.

There was a black market in a wide range of other things during the war – including clothing and even military equipment.

Cheeky Chad

A little chap who turned up everywhere during the war was Chad. (The Americans had a character just like him called Kilroy.) You'd find his picture daubed all over the place as graffiti.

Chad was a bald-headed little fellow looking over a wall, with just his clutching fingers and his eyes showing.

The message on the wall below him always began 'Wot, no . . .', and he kept people's spirits up in a world blighted by shortages.

WOT, NO SWEETS?

Here are a few of the things that Lord Woolton's cooks recommended to the hard-pressed British housewife:

- pilchard tart
- fish-and-cabbage-spread sandwiches
- dripping cake
- crumb fudge (for using up stale crusts)
- eggless batter (for coating fish).

There were a lot more recipes like that which you could find by thumbing through the ministry's *Food Facts* booklet or by listening to the regular BBC radio programme, *The Kitchen Front*.

If you have the sort of great-grandparents who urge you to eat potatoes without peeling them and to munch the leafy tops of carrots and turnips because they're good for you — well, you have to forgive them for learning their disgusting habits during the war.

Wartime recipes

You had to make the best of what you had in a Blitz kitchen. Here are two recipes by Marguerite Patten, who was a 'home economist' (cookery expert) at the Ministry of Food.

• Woolton pie
(named after the minister for food)

Ingredients:
- 1 lb (454 g) each of diced potatoes, cauliflower, swedes and carrots
- three or four spring onions
- one teaspoonful of vegetable extract
- 1oz (28 g) of oatmeal or rolled oats.

Method:
- Dice and cook the potatoes, cauliflower, swedes and carrots in boiling salted water.
- Strain, but keep ¾ pint (425 ml) of the vegetable water.
- Arrange the vegetables in a large pie dish or casserole. Add the vegetable extract and the rolled oats or oatmeal to the vegetable liquid. Cook until thickened and pour over the vegetables.
- Chop and add the spring onions.
- Allow to cool, and cover with a crust of potato or wheatmeal pastry. Bake in a moderate oven and serve with a brown gravy.

• Eggless sponge

Ingredients:
- 6 oz (170 g) self-raising flour with one level teaspoon of baking powder; or 6 oz (170 g) plain flour with three level teaspoons of baking powder
- 2½ oz (70 g) margarine
- 2 oz (60 g) sugar
- 1 level tablespoon golden syrup
- ¼ pint (140 ml) milk, or milk and water
- jam for filling.

Method:
- Sift the flour and baking powder. Cream the margarine, sugar and golden syrup until soft and light, add a little flour, then a little liquid.
- Continue like this until you have a smooth mixture. Grease and flour two 7 in (18 cm) sandwich tins and divide the mixture between the two. Bake for approximately 20 minutes or until firm to touch, just above the centre of a moderately hot oven.
- Turn out and sandwich with jam.

Apart from the recipes, Lord W. had a team of people dreaming up slogans. Here are a few of them:

- Waste not, want not.
- Food is a munition of war – don't waste it.
- Save kitchen waste for the pigs.
- Doctor Carrot – the children's best friend.

Yes, they were obsessed with carrots, which 'keep you healthy and help you see in the blackout'.[1] It was the most plentiful vegetable (in fact there was a glut of them at one time), so it made good sense to promote them – although you might not have enjoyed some of the recipes they suggested:

- carrot marmalade
- carrot fudge
- carrolade (a home-made drink using carrot and swede juice).

Dr Carrot's best friend was Potato Pete, who had his own (very popular) song.

---

1. *Any truth in that? Not much. Carrots contain vitamin A, which is good for your eyes and skin – but eat too many of them and you'll not only feel very unwell but will turn a nasty shade of orange, too!*

Families had two waste bins. One was for tins and bottles, and the other for potato peelings and any vegetable tops you weren't actually eating – these became food for chickens and a growing population of healthily fat pigs. (Let's hope they were grateful.)

You threw away as little as possible during the war. 'Up housewives and at 'em!' read one poster. 'Put out your paper, metal, bones – they make planes, guns, tanks, ships and ammunition.'

Did anyone ever ask them how they did that?

Threadbare Britain

And have you ever wondered why so many women are pictured wearing headscarves during the war? That's right – they couldn't find a decent hat anywhere!

In fact the material for new clothes of any kind was very hard to come by, and if you heard that something you wanted had arrived in the shops you rushed along there and probably had to stand in a queue for hours.

The Empress's New Nylons

If you saw a smart young lady going out in the evening in what looked like a fashionable pair of nylon stockings, you were probably being fooled.

Nylons were extremely hard to get, so some women painted their legs with gravy browning and ran a false seam up the back with an eyebrow pencil.

The gravy did pong a bit in hot weather!

It looks quite convincing in the blackout.

You had to queue for food, too. Have you ever noticed that in many other countries people jostle one another in a kind of running battle when they all want the same thing, whereas in Britain we have the habit of patiently standing in line?

We've the Blitz to thank for that. It taught us the virtue (and the boredom) of queuing.

But if your clothes wore out and you couldn't find a replacement, the answer was 'Make Do and Mend' – one of the most famous of all wartime slogans.

As with the food recipes, the government had loads of ideas about making a little go a long way. (We call it recycling now, don't we?)

- Unpick worn-out pullovers and use the wool to make a new one or to darn socks.
- Turn old curtains into shirts and dresses.
- Dye sheets or blankets to make curtains.
- 'Turn' worn sheets by cutting them in half and sewing the edges together.

Married in a parachute

All clothes were mended and altered as much as possible in wartime, and most people accepted that – but what if you had a special occasion, such as a wedding?

A prized material, if you could get it, was the silk from an airman's parachute. Of course you'd have to make the dress yourself or get a friend to do it, but that kind of skill was much more common in those days.

Once the parachute had been separated into its individual panels, a skilled dressmaker would have her work cut out to make the most of the precious material. Nothing would be wasted: little bits left over from the dress could become luxurious lingerie.

Would most brides keep the dress for ever as a memento? Possibly not, because there were further demands on the material – when the time came, it might make an excellent christening gown!

Sylvia spots the dress of her dreams.

Tiresome toys

Although children could happily ignore shortages of things like petrol – and positively rejoice in the rationing of soap – they can't have been too pleased about the quality of toys on offer.

Of course they never dreamt about the electronic gadgets we fill the house with today, but even by the standards of the time they couldn't expect a bumper haul for Christmas. 'Thanks for the knitted woollen doll, auntie!'

The more resourceful made their own amusements. Here are a few, based on wartime memories:

- Stilts from empty tins. Knock two holes under the rims of a pair of empty tins, pass string through them and walk on the tins, drawing your feet up with the string.

- Tyre fights. Find tyres large enough for boys to crouch inside, and then wheel them at running speed against each other with the intention of knocking opposing tyres over. (Don't try this one at home.)

- Tiddlywinks football. Draw the shape of a pitch on the front-room carpet with a piece of chalk (better not try this one either!); use one tiddlywink for the ball and take it in turns to flick it towards your opponent's goal.

- Kick-can. This is a form of hide-and-seek. Find an old tin can. One of you kicks it away, and while the person whose turn it is goes to fetch it, everybody else runs away and hides.

Another free amusement was collecting shrapnel and other fragments of Blitz memorabilia. The high temperatures caused by explosions sometimes produced beautiful rainbow colours on the metal.

Youngsters would swap and trade items like these, keeping them in brown paper bags. (There were no plastic carriers in those days.)

The biggest prize of all was to own an unexploded incendiary bomb. Some of these were no bigger than a policeman's truncheon, and quite easy to hide – though if an adult found out about it, there'd be ructions!

Your parents, though, were probably far too busy doing other things to notice.

If your mother wasn't working in a factory or running around on WRVS duties, she was probably unpicking old cardigans, queuing in a shop or boiling up bones for a stew.

As for your father, if he wasn't serving in the armed forces, working in a reserved occupation or patrolling the streets as an ARP warden, you'd probably find him down the garden or in a field, with his sleeves rolled up and wearing a stout pair of wellington boots.

Making do and mending

CHAPTER EIGHT

DIGGING FOR VICTORY

German bombs and U-boats had stopped the flow of food coming into Britain. Why did this matter? Because at the outbreak of war Britain wasn't producing nearly enough food of her own – it had been cheaper to buy it from other countries.

- As much as 90 per cent of the fats and cereals consumed in Britain came from abroad.
- More than 50 per cent of Britain's meat was imported, too.
- And most British livestock – sheep, cattle, pigs – was fattened on imported feed.

DIG FOR VICTORY

Frank puts his back into it on the allotment.

Faced with famine, the government acted with a speed we'd find hard to imagine today.

It aimed to have an extra 1,700,000 acres (688,000 heactares – that's the equivalent of about a million football pitches) ready for production by harvest time 1940 – and it reached this target as early as April.

Farmers were given a cash incentive to plough up more of their land, and many worked through the night as well as during every available hour of daylight.

Plough Now!

As you'd expect, there were plenty of slogans to encourage people to do their bit. Farmers were told that they would have their land taken over, or 'requisitioned', if they didn't become more productive, but the 'Plough Now!' campaign involved every community in the country.

All counties appointed War Agricultural Committees (commonly known as War Ags), and their job was to find as much spare land as possible to grow vegetables and cereals.

And who would do the digging? Every spare man and woman in the country.

'We want not only the big man with the plough,' said the Minister for Agriculture, Rob Hudson, in October 1939, 'but the little man with the spade to get busy this autumn. Let *Dig for Victory* be the motto of everyone with a garden.'

First coined by the *Evening Standard* newspaper, this was perhaps the most famous wartime slogan of all.

Of course, you had to plan what you planted rather carefully. If you had a bumper crop of parsnips, say, or cauliflowers, you could end up having to eat the same vegetable every day for weeks.

But people were soon growing runner beans, Brussels sprouts, peas, carrots, potatoes and cabbages all over the place, quite apart from in their gardens and allotments.

Here's a selection of unlikely places :

- parks and recreation grounds
- tennis courts
- golf courses
- the roofs of Anderson shelters
- bomb sites
- railway embankments.

One in five homes had an allotment, and these back-garden areas were eventually producing a million tonnes of vegetables a year. Special allotments were created for children, so that they got the growing habit.

Royalty sets an example

Nowhere was sacred when it came to growing more food. The royal family, for instance, turned over Windsor Great Park to the growing of wheat and created a vegetable patch in one of the herbaceous borders at Buckingham Palace. Vegetables were also grown just outside the palace, in the beds surrounding the Victoria Memorial, as well as in the moat at the Tower of London.

Walt Disney *lends* a hand

We've already met Dr. Carrot (page 126). Now's the time to introduce you to three more members of his family, all of them invented for the Ministry of Food by the famous American maker of cartoon films, Walt Disney.

These were Pop Carrot, Clara Carrot and Carroty George. Here's what people were told about George when being given a simple recipe:

'You can meet young Carroty George any day at the Hot Pot if you're a member. He belongs, of course, to all the best clubs, and what's more he has the entrée of all the best kitchens. That's because he's a fellow of tact and resource and can so quickly adapt himself to any occasion, sweet or savoury. See how well he fits into:

• Carrot Hot Pot

'Wash and coarsely grate 6 carrots and 6 potatoes; mix with 2 tablespoons packet sage and onion. Make seasoning of 2 teaspoons salt, ½ teaspoon pepper, and, if possible, brown sugar.

'Put half the vegetables in a stewpot, cover with half the seasoning, add rest of vegetables and rest of seasoning. No water required, cover stewpot and bake very slowly for 2 hours. You'll have a dish very much out of the ordinary, for 3 or 4.'

Here are a few tips from one of the government's many brochures:

- Women must help. They make good gardeners and can do much of the work – getting the older children to help them.

- Onions have been as rare as diamonds. Potatoes, too, have at times been scarce. Make sure of getting them by growing them yourself.

- Every row of potatoes – every row of cabbage – helps your family and your country. Flowers add nothing to the nation's 'growing' power.

- To grow vegetables for winter and summer you must have a plan – or you will have a summer glut and bare ground all the winter. A simple plan is yours for the asking.

- Thousands of people have discovered that a 10-rod [0.025-hectare] plot will keep a family of five in vegetables for eight months of the year.

- Food is just as important a weapon of war as guns.

The war's 'celebrity gardener' was C. H. Middleton, who broadcast on the BBC's Home Service just before lunch every Sunday.

Three million people tuned in. The use of his initials may sound a bit stuffy today, but when the government brought out his *Digging for Victory* book to encourage vegetable growing he became simply 'Mr Middleton'.

The garden farmyard

If you had any spare room in your garden once you'd dug a plot for vegetables, it was time to think about getting some pigs, chickens, rabbits or goats.

The government – of course – had booklets to help you, and *Keeping Poultry and Rabbits on Scraps* was a favourite.

'There is no known waste from human edible food which is harmful in moderation,' wrote its authors.

'Do not be content with using your own scraps; get others to save for you. There are plenty of people too busily occupied, or maybe some too lazy and unpatriotic, to exert themselves and undertake any work of national importance.'

A Dig for Victory song

(*This is one that Vera Lynn didn't sing.*)

Dig! Dig! Dig! And your muscles will grow big.
Keep on pushing the spade –
Don't mind the worms,
Just ignore their squirms,
And when your back aches laugh with glee
And keep on diggin'
Till we give our foes a wiggin'*
Dig! dig! dig! to victory.

* a telling-off – meaning, with classic British understatement, a defeat.

A wartime ditty

Those who have the will to win,
Cook potatoes in their skin,
Knowing that the sight of peelings
Deeply hurts Lord Woolton's feelings.

The Women's Land Army

In 1939 Lady Denman, the first national chairman of the Women's Institute, began to organise a new workforce to take the place of farmworkers enlisting in the armed forces.

The government tried to make life in the Women's Land Army sound glamorous, but if you left your home in the city to live far away in a run-down farmworker's cottage with no running water, gas or electricity, you might have disagreed.

Some 80,000 women eventually signed up to a poorly paid 48 hours a week in winter and 50 hours in summer. They wore a uniform of green jerseys, brown breeches and brown felt hats. Here are a few of the things they found themselves doing:

- milking cows
- ploughing fields
- planting crops
- digging up potatoes
- harvesting fruit
- haymaking
- threshing
- killing rats.

There was also a special Timber Corps, whose members – known as Lumber Jills (rather than lumberjacks: a terrible joke) – cut down trees and worked in sawmills.

At the beginning of the war a lot of people laughed at the idea of young 'slips of girls' doing men's work on the farms. By the time it was all over, the union representing farm workers was urging them to stay!

The teenage Princess Elizabeth – the future Queen Elizabeth II – was the WLA's patron during the war. In her Christmas message to all serving Land Girls in 1941 she said they had earned the right to think of themselves as an army. Their skill and devotion, she told them, had 'released great battalions of men who now fight for the land they formerly tilled'.

• Chickens

Hens were popular, because they didn't require too much attention and would give you lovely fresh eggs. You could also eat the chickens themselves later on, although many people felt too attached to them for that – they'd become pets.

By the end of the war the Domestic Poultry Keepers' Council had well over a million members owning 12 million birds.

To feed them you could get special poultry-mash ration coupons – but only if you gave up part of your normal egg ration first.

But this was only fair. A single chicken might give you 180 eggs during its first laying season, and if you had half a dozen of them you would end up with far more eggs than you could possibly buy in the shops.

' **F**ood is just as
important a weapon
of war as guns.'

Government advice leaflet

• **Rabbits**

You could feed rabbits common weeds as well as scraps, and it's well known that they breed like... well, like rabbits!

By joining the local rabbit club, you qualified for a bran ration, but there were government regulations here, too. You were supposed to offer half of your brood to the local butcher – although how he knew the size of your new 'family' is anyone's guess.

fit for human consumption

If you have a *whale* of an appetite you can eat like a *horse* – but imagine tucking into either of those things for supper!

Well, the government encouraged people to do just that in wartime, and some of them reluctantly gave it a try – once.

In Britain, horsemeat had traditionally been sold as dog food, so butchers had to put signs up saying 'Fit for human consumption'.

Rabbit Dumplings

Here's a recipe from *Food Facts from the Kitchen Front*, which had a foreword by Lord Woolton:

'If you haven't tried rabbit before, now's the time – it has a 'gamey' flavour all its own!

- '2–3 fleshy joints of cooked rabbit – also the broth in which they were cooked
- scraps of bacon if possible
- 8 oz [230 g] self raising flour
- 2 oz [60 g] chopped suet, finely chopped
- water to mix

'Remove the meat from the joint and chop finely. Sieve the flour into a basin, add a pinch of salt, the suet and the prepared meat with finely chopped bacon if available.

'Mix with a little water to make a stiff paste and form into small dumplings with floured fingers. Boil these in the broth in which the rabbit was cooked, keeping the lid on the pan. Serve broth and dumplings together.'

• **Pigs**

Not many town gardens were suitable for pigs, although some people did fatten their own porkers on vegetable scraps in the back yard.

The easiest solution was to join a pig club. There were some 7,000 of them throughout the country. People banded together to buy a number of pigs and look after them, and when they were slaughtered (a big occasion for everybody) half of the carcasses had to be sold to the government.

The rest were, of course, shared between club members as pork or bacon, although – as you'll have guessed by now – you had to sacrifice a bit of your meat ration to make up for it.

You'll also have guessed that people often tried to get round these rules so that they could make themselves some money on the black market.

One man reared three pigs instead of the two he'd told the authorities about, and he had the third cut up into portions so that he could sell them for a profit. He waited until darkness had fallen and then put them into a baby's pram and wheeled them round the town.

'You're out late with that baby,' a policeman said, crossing the road.

'Trying to get him off to sleep,' the man said quickly, thinking on his feet – and watched in relief as the officer turned on his heel and walked away.

They call that telling porkies!

He's got a bit of a snuffle.

The Blitz in Britain

There is not space here to show all the locations bombed by the Luftwaffe. These are some of the towns that suffered particularly heavy bombing.

Greenock
Glasgow
Clydebank
Belfast
Newcastle
Sunderland
Barrow-in-Furness
York
Hull
Bootle
Liverpool
Sheffield
Manchester
Nottingham
Norwich
Birmingham
Coventry
Colchester
Swansea
Cardiff
Swindon
Southend
Canterbury
Bristol & Avonmouth
London
Margate
Ramsgate
Bath
Dover
Folkestone
Plymouth
Exeter
Southampton
Portsmouth
Brighton
Eastbourne
Hastings

CHAPTER NINE

BLITZED BRITAIN

Londoners may have suffered the brunt of the bombing, but millions of other people throughout the British Isles experienced the full horror of the German onslaught. Here are a few figures for the number of air raids by the end of 1940 alone:

- **London 126**
- **Liverpool 60**
- **Birmingham 36**
- **Coventry 31**
- **Plymouth 13**
- **Portsmouth 13**

In London you could expect raids every night. Elsewhere? You just never knew when.

Ports in peril

The obvious targets were the ports, with their ships, their warehouses, their grain stores, their railway sidings and the clusters of factories which huddled around them.

Sure enough, the Luftwaffe hammered such towns and cities relentlessly: from Merseyside in the north-west to Hull, Newcastle and Sunderland in the north-east; from Clydeside in Scotland and Belfast in Northern Ireland to Cardiff and Swansea in Wales; along the south coast of England west from Dover through Southampton, Portsmouth and Plymouth round to Bristol.

A school playground rhyme from Bristol

Under the spreading chestnut tree
Neville Chamberlain said to me,
'If you want to get your gas masks free,
Join the blinking ARP!'

The government wanted to hide from the Germans just how devastating their attacks had been, so they ensured that there was only a limited reporting of them in the newspapers and on the BBC.

Some of the smaller towns well away from London, such as Plymouth, hadn't expected to be in the firing line at all, and they now had to rush through evacuation programmes for their children.

• **Liverpool and Merseyside**
The River Mersey was vital to Britain's war effort. Its quays stretched for all of 11 miles (18 km), and around 90 per cent of all the country's imports came across the Atlantic to Liverpool and its neighbouring docks.

The area received vicious attacks during the first week of May 1941 – the worst known outside London – when half the docks were put out of action.

Nearby Bootle, a small town next to the docks, was devastated by the 'May Blitz'. Only 15 per cent of its houses survived.

Lest we forget

St Luke's church in Liverpool city centre was destroyed by an incendiary bomb on 5 May 1941, but its walls remained standing.

Today it's the focal point of a garden of remembrance to commemorate the thousands of local men, women and children who died as a result of the bombing of their city and region.

Here are the terrible figures for Liverpool during that week alone:

- 1,453 people killed
- 1,065 seriously injured
- 4,400 houses destroyed
- 51,000 people made homeless.

But one disaster wasn't caused by the Germans at all. The SS *Malakand*, which was berthed in Huskisson Dock with a huge cargo of bombs, was set alight when a barrage balloon drifted free and collided with it.

There was an almighty blast, which not only destroyed the dock and the surrounding quays but carried some pieces of the ship's plating into a park more than a mile (1.6 km) away.

- Hull

The north-east, because of the docks on Tyneside and elsewhere, was one of the worst-hit areas after London. Hull was attacked over and over again.

There were 92,660 houses in Hull before the Blitz. How many do you think were left intact once the bombing was over?

Just 5,945. Some 1,200 people were killed, and 152,000 were temporarily made homeless.

Hull, incidentally, has a curious claim to fame – it received the *first* daylight raid of the war and the *last* air raid involving piloted aircraft rather than V-1s and V-2s.

• **Bristol**

The River Avon marked an easy route for Luftwaffe pilots, guiding them upstream from the coast to Bristol with its harbour and – perhaps more significantly – the Bristol Aeroplane factory, turning out the fighter planes which would attempt to see them off.

During the worst months of the Blitz the city had 919 tonnes of high-explosive bombs dropped on it, with devastating results:

• **1,299 people were killed.**
• **1,303 were seriously injured.**
• **697 were rescued from debris.**
• **81,830 houses were destroyed.**

The biggest bomb ever dropped on Bristol, on 4 January 1941, was later nicknamed 'Satan'. It was 2.4 m long, not counting the tail, and weighed all of 1,815 kg. Fortunately it didn't explode, but it was more than two years before a bomb disposal crew got it out of the ground – having dug down nearly 9 metres to find it.

The relic was so impressive that it was paraded through the streets of London during the Victory in Europe parade at the end of the war.

'Cat's Eyes' Cunningham

During the Blitz the British brought out a new night-fighter plane, the Bristol Beaufighter.

In early 1941 it was provided with an improved radar system, which allowed pilots to 'see' the enemy with the aid of bounced-back radio waves.

This was top secret, so the best-known fighter pilot of the war, John Cunningham, was credited with having superb natural vision.

They called him 'Cat's Eyes' Cunningham!

• Plymouth

The royal dockyards were the chief target in Plymouth, but that didn't prevent catastrophic damage in the city centre, which was largely destroyed.

Although the population was 220,000 at the outbreak of war, there would sometimes be little more than half that number when the bombs fell. Not only had many of the children been evacuated, but when a raid was expected thousands of people would be taken by lorry into the Devon countryside, often to the fringes of Dartmoor.

Resurgam!

There's a granite plaque above the entrance to St Andrew's parish church in Plymouth with the Latin word *Resurgam* (meaning 'I shall rise again') carved into it.

This replaces a wooden sign which a defiant local headmistress nailed over the door immediately after the church was badly damaged in the Blitz.

During 59 bombing attacks on Plymouth, 1,172 civilians were killed and 4,448 people were injured.

flattening the factories

The industrial cities of the north of England and the Midlands were working non-stop for the war effort, and it was obvious that they would be ruthlessly targeted by the Luftwaffe.

So it was that Manchester, Sheffield, Birmingham and Coventry were deluged with as much 'heavy metal' as the enemy could contrive to drop on them.

• **Sheffield**
The Germans called their attack on Britain's steel-making city Operation Crucible. It took place on two December nights in 1941 – and it was deadly:

- **660 people were killed.**
- **1,500 were injured.**
- **40,000 were made homeless.**
- **3,000 homes were demolished.**
- **A further 3,000 homes were badly damaged.**

No fewer than six George Medals were awarded to citizens of Sheffield for their bravery during these raids.

The king and queen toured the city soon afterwards in order to inspect the damage and boost morale among the survivors.

Winston Churchill came, too – touring the blitzed city, addressing a crowd of 20,000 in Town Hall Square and giving his familiar 'V for victory' hand sign.

• Coventry
One of the problems for the people of Coventry was that the munitions factories targeted by the German bombers sat cheek-by-jowl with areas of housing.

They couldn't hit one without destroying the other – even if they'd wanted to.

When it came, on 14 November 1940, the devastation of Coventry was so great that German propaganda chief Goebbels coined the word *coventriert* – 'Coventried' – to describe a place that had been laid waste.

Coventry Cathedral in 1940
(compare page 174)

163

Did Churchill know?

It's been suggested that the clever people at Bletchley Park (see page 89) unscrambled German messages which revealed that Coventry was about to be attacked – but that Winston Churchill decided to do nothing about it.

According to this theory, Churchill made no special effort to defend the city because the Germans would then have realised that the British had cracked their Enigma codes.

This needed to be kept secret from them so that Britain could continue to use the coded information in order to win the war.

Many people who worked at Bletchley Park have denied the story. They say the prime minister *did* sometimes ignore the information they gave him in order to fool the Germans, but that he simply didn't know about the Coventry raid in time.

This is now the accepted version of events. But what would you have done in Churchill's shoes if you *had* been told about the raid in advance?

The German code-name for this assault was the innocent-sounding Moonlight Sonata.

Coventry Cathedral was completely gutted and the city centre flattened as the Germans dropped more than 30,000 incendiary bombs, nearly 900 incendiary canisters and 500 tonnes of high-explosive bombs.

The raid lasted for 12 hours, killing at least 568 people (the official total) and seriously wounding 1,200 more.

The 'Baedeker Blitz'

Some other British cities were attacked for another reason altogether – revenge.

This is not a happy story. After the Americans entered the war at the end of 1941, the Allies had much more equipment and were able to bomb German cities with a new ferocity.

A policy of so-called 'strategic bombing' began the following year. It meant choosing targets that would weaken German morale.

The very first of these raids was on the medieval Baltic city of Lübeck, which on the night of 28 March was practically destroyed, with the loss of about a thousand lives.

There was outrage in Germany. Baron Gustav Braun von Sturm, a Nazi propagandist, is reported to have said, 'We shall go out and bomb every building in Britain marked with three stars in the Baedeker Guide.'

Two German pilots

Ernst von Kugel took part in the first raid on Exeter, and this is what he said later:

'It was a night of terror for the Exeter people. Over the town I saw whole streets of houses on fire. Flames burst out of windows and doors, devouring the roofs.

'We thought of the thousands of men, women and children, the victims of our deadly visit, but we thought of our Führer [Hitler] and the command he gave: "Revenge!" With cold calculation we carried out our orders.'

(Express and Echo, *Exeter*)

Willi Schludecker, who flew a Dornier during the Baedeker Blitz, came to Britain more than 60 years later to apologise for his part in it.

'The war was madness,' he said. 'I was afraid the British would be very angry, but I find that now they are very gentle.

'We were told what to do and we did it, just like the young British pilots.'

167

The Battle of the Beams

One exciting Second World War battle couldn't be seen at all!

The Germans invented a clever guidance system for the Luftwaffe. This involved radio beams which crossed above their planned targets in Britain.

Pilots would fly along one beam and release their bombs when they picked up the signal from a second one.

When the British countered this by emitting 'spoiler signals' on the same frequencies, the Germans designed an even more sophisticated system – and so the battle went on.

BBC engineers played a large part in its final stages. Their television transmitters had been idle since the service was closed down at the beginning of the war, but now they were switched on to beam the German signals back at their own aircraft and confuse their instruments.

The famous Baedeker series of tourist guides features the culture travellers can expect to enjoy – castles, cathedrals and so on. German bombers were now going to attack Britain's beautiful old cities in reprisal.

Bath, Canterbury, Exeter, Norwich and York were all targeted. More than 1,600 people were killed and 50,000 buildings destroyed.

• Exeter
The first of these raids was directed at Exeter, which was to have two more 'Baedeker' visits for good measure, and which was attacked a total of 19 times throughout the war.

A few Exeter figures:

- 265 people were killed.
- 1,809 homes were lost to residents.
- 400 other buildings were totally destroyed.
- 9 churches were destroyed.
- 1,000,000 library books were lost.

'Exeter was the jewel of the west. We have destroyed that jewel, and the Luftwaffe will return to finish the job.'
German radio report, 4 May 1942

You might think library books aren't that important, but it's a useful reminder of how the ordinary things we value can disappear in a time of war.

Coastal raids

You didn't have to live near a port, in an industrial city or in a Baedeker town to fear the German guns.

Brighton, on the south coast, has its share of cultural attractions (including the famous Royal Pavilion), but it took a beating partly because it was such a handy target on the route to London.

'Some chicken'

Winston Churchill addressed the Canadian Parliament on 30 December 1941:

'When I warned them [the French] that Britain would fight on alone whatever they did, their generals told their prime minister and his divided cabinet, "In three weeks England will have her neck wrung like a chicken."

'Some chicken! Some neck!'

Sometimes there would be raids specifically aimed at the town (with its railway works and gasholder singled out for attack), and on these occasions fighter planes might strafe the streets with machine-gun fire as pedestrians desperately dived for cover.

At other times, though, planes returning from a raid on London would simply drop their leftover bombs as they passed in order to lighten the load and so speed their journey home across the Channel.

Several towns east of Brighton and round into Kent and Essex suffered in this way, among them Eastbourne, Hastings, Folkestone, Ramsgate, Margate and Southend.

Once Hitler had begun to concentrate his attacks against Russia on the Eastern Front, it was clear that an invasion of Britain was unlikely. But until the war was over the beaches were still covered in barbed wire and tank traps, so the inhabitants of these coastal towns continued to think of themselves as being in the front line of the war against Germany.

The end at last!

And so the chicken, as Churchill had forecast, did *not* have its neck wrung.

On 30 April 1945 Hitler committed suicide in his Berlin bunker, and a week later the German Supreme Command surrendered.

May 8 was celebrated in Britain as VE (Victory in Europe) Day – although the war was not finally over until Japan surrendered some months later, on 14 August.

'This is your hour,' Churchill told the people of Britain in a VE-Day broadcast from 10 Downing Street. 'This is your victory.'

They responded in a way that was to shock and hurt him...

VE-Day celebrations outside Buckingham Palace

Coventry today: the new
cathedral amongst the
ruins of the old

(compare page 163)

CHAPTER TEN

A NEW BEGINNING

They called it 'the khaki election', after the colour of a soldier's uniform. In July 1945 millions of Britons went to the polls in a general election – and brought about an amazing revolution. Conservative leader Winston Churchill had been confident of victory, but instead the Labour Party swept to power with a huge majority. What on earth had happened?

What had happened was that soldiers returned from the war, working-class people bombed out of their flimsy houses, women who had had a rare taste of independence through their wartime work – these and a great many others decided that it was time for a change. They weren't going to be pushed around any more. Hadn't they won the war? Well, now they would win the peace.

In its manifesto (its declaration of what it would do if it was elected) the Labour Party said the bloodshed of the First World War had led to no improvements in the life of ordinary men and women.

'Never,' the manifesto read – cleverly echoing Churchill's comment on the Battle of Britain – 'was so much injury done to so many by so few.'

This time it would be different. Labour was a socialist party, believing that the government should control (or 'nationalise') many things which private companies had run before.

Here are some of the things they took over:

- gas
- coal
- electricity
- the railways
- the Bank of England.

Two pieces of wit
- and a big mistake

Clement Attlee, the leader of the Labour Party, was a shy and quiet man, and the larger-than-life Winston Churchill enjoyed making fun of him whenever the opportunity arose.

He once referred to him as 'a sheep in sheep's clothing'.

And on another occasion he described Attlee as 'a modest little man with much to be modest about'.

But Churchill made a big mistake when he said that a new Labour government would need to set up 'some form of Gestapo' in order to carry out its socialist policies.

Attlee seized on this slur. The public would now understand 'how great is the difference between Winston Churchill the great leader, in war, of a united nation, and Mr Churchill, the party leader of the Conservatives'.

Attlee went on to win the election hands down.

The first banana

Many people remember eating their first banana when, at last, supplies of fruit picked up again.

One lad who had been brought up on a cherry farm thought they must be the same kind of thing: he threw away what he found inside and tried to eat the skin!

The novelist Evelyn Waugh behaved dreadfully when his wife came home with bananas for their three children, who had never eaten one before.

He took all three, peeled and cut them, poured cream and sugar on top – and then proceeded to eat the lot while they watched.

'He was permanently marked down in my estimation,' wrote his son Auberon years later.

'From that moment, I never treated anything he had to say on faith or morals very seriously.'

Of course the new government made many mistakes, as governments always do, and Winston Churchill would one day become prime minister again, but the Labour Party made many important changes.

• The National Health Service
We take it for granted today, but the launch of the NHS in July 1948 for the first time brought treatment 'free to all at the point of delivery'. It's changed quite a bit since then, and we often grumble about it, but no politician would dare try to do away with it.

• Housing
There was a massive housing shortage after the war. Not only had so many houses been bombed into rubble – more than three million of them in all – but many who had gone to war as young men, now came back all these years later looking for their first home in which to start a new family life.

One solution was the erection of 150,000 'prefabs' – prefabricated houses assembled where they were needed, often by German and Italian prisoners of war.

The birth of the National Health Service

And so it was that the toddler we saw being snatched from a north London window at the beginning of this book spent his childhood and teens in a south London prefab.

I can still recall my mother's squeal of delight on discovering that the kitchen contained what we would today regard as a very tiny fridge. This was an unbelievable luxury in what – also unbelievably – was a home of her very own.

For Mum and for millions like her, we had come through!

Glossary

allotment A small piece of public land rented by a private individual for growing vegetables.

appeasement The prewar policy of agreeing to Hitler's demands in the hope of avoiding war.

billet To accommodate people such as soldiers or evacuees in civilians' houses.

call-up papers The official notice sent to those who had been conscripted.

camouflage To hide something by making it blend in with its surroundings.

censor To prohibit the release of information that might be useful to an enemy; also, the official who does this.

concentration camp A camp in which civilian prisoners are held under armed guard.

conscript To require a person to join the armed forces; also, a person who has been conscripted.

cryptanalyst A code-breaker.

enlist To join the armed forces.

evacuate To move people or goods to a place of safety.

evacuee A person, usually a child, who is evacuated.

extermination camp A Nazi concentration camp in which Jews and others were systematically killed.

incendiary bomb A bomb designed to cause fires.

Kindertransport A scheme for evacuating Jewish children from Nazi Germany and German-occupied countries.

Luftwaffe The German air force.

morale Confidence or optimism.

Nazi Party The National Socialist Party, founded by Adolf Hitler, which governed Germany from 1933 to 1945. Its policies included the extermination of Jews and others whom it considered to be 'undesirable'.

non-combatant Any person in a war zone who is not a fighting member of the armed forces.

occupied Invaded and governed by an enemy country.

oz. Short for 'ounce', a unit of weight equal to 28.35 g.

pogrom An organised riot against Jewish people.

prefab A prefabricated building – one that can be assembled quickly on site from parts made in a factory. Prefab homes built in the 1940s were meant to last only a few years, but some of them are still in use.

propaganda Any kind of publication or broadcast that is intended to change peoples' opinions in favour of a particular point of view.

RAF The British Royal Air Force.

rationing A system for sharing out goods fairly when they are in short supply.

requisition To take something for military or official use, not necessarily with the owner's permission.

reserved occupation A job which is so important that those who do it are exempt from being conscripted.

respirator The official term for a gas mask.

shrapnel Fragments of metal from an exploded bomb or shell.

strafe To shoot from the air with machine-guns.

subsidise To pay for something partly with public money, to ensure that those who need it can afford it.

synagogue A Jewish place of worship.

U-boat A German submarine, from the German word *Unterseeboot*.

Blitz timeline

1938

September 30 Chamberlain's 'Peace for our time' speech. Germany occupies Sudetenland.

November 9–10 *Kristallnacht* pogrom.

December 2 First *Kindertransport* children reach Britain.

1939

March Germany occupies rest of Czechoslovakia; Britain promises to protect Poland if it is attacked.

June RAF producing 750 planes per month.

August Royal Navy mobilised; reserves called up.

   31 Evacuation of children begins.

September 1 Last *Kindertransport* children leave Germany for Britain.

   3 War declared; first air-raid warning, near Croydon.

   22 Petrol rationed.

October 10 Women's Land Army recruitment suspended after 500,000 enrol.

December 2 Conscription extended to all men between 19 and 41.

1940

January 8 Butter, sugar and bacon rationed.

February 12 Paper rationed.

March 3 National Savings announce £100m invested since start of war.

   11 Meat rationed.

April 3 Lord Woolton appointed Minister of Food.

   30 First civilian deaths when German plane crashes in Clacton.

May 8 Chamberlain resigns.

10 Churchill becomes Prime Minister.

13 Churchill offers 'blood, sweat and tears'.

14 Local Defence Volunteers (LDV) announced. Last *Kindertransport* children leave the Netherlands for Britain.

22 Emergency Powers Act passed.

26 Dunkirk evacuation begins (ends June 4).

27 Butter rations cut.

June 4 Churchill's 'We shall fight them' speech.

5 Strikes are banned.

17 Churchill's 'Finest hour' speech.

July 11 Beaverbrook makes public appeal for aluminium.

20 Buying and selling new cars is banned.

23 LDV becomes Home Guard. Emergency budget imposes higher taxes on luxury goods.

August 12 First German shell lands on Dover.

20 Churchill's 'Never was so much owed' speech.

24 First bombing raid on London.

26 Portsmouth bombed.

28 Liverpool bombed.

September 6 Armed forces put on 'yellow alert' for invasion within three days.

7 London Blitz begins.

10 School flattened in West Ham, with heavy loss of life. Buckingham Palace hit by a bomb.

17 *City of Benares* sunk with evacuee children on board.

21 Underground stations allowed to be used as bomb shelters.

October 9 St Paul's Cathedral bombed.

21 200th air raid on Liverpool.

November 14 Coventry bombed.

30 Southampton bombed.

December 3 Extra rations of tea and sugar for Christmas.

  30 'Landmark' buildings hit in heavy raid on London.

  31 Firewatching becomes compulsory.

1941

January 4 Huge bomb 'Satan' dropped on Bristol.

February 9 Churchill's 'Give us the tools' speech.

March 17 Jam and marmalade rationed.

April 19 Essential Work Order for women.

  21–24 Plymouth heavily bombed.

May 1–7 Heavy bombing of Liverpool. Glasgow bombed.

  8 Newcastle and Plymouth bombed.

  10–11 Worst bombing of London.

  23 House of Commons hit.

June 22 Churchill promises to aid USSR.

December 4 Umarried women aged 20–30 called up.

  7 Japanese attack Pearl Harbor.

  8 United States enters the war.

  12–13 Sheffield bombed.

1942

February 9 Soap rationed.

March 5 Conscription extended to men aged 40, women 20–30.

  11 New law means black marketeers face up to 14 years in prison. National Loaf replaces white bread.

April 23 First 'Baedeker raid', on Exeter.

June 1 Fripperies banned on clothing.

  3 Government takes over coal mines.

  6 Undetected bomb explodes at Elephant & Castle, London.

July 26 Sweets and chocolates rationed.

August 10 Colchester raided.

19 Dieppe Raid: 907 Canadian soldiers killed, 1,874 captured.

31 Utility furniture introduced.

October 23 – November 5 Battle of El Alamein.

December 1 Beveridge Report outlines plans for a postwar National Health Service (NHS).

16 German hit-and-run raids on 20 southern towns.

1943

March 3 Bethnal Green tube disaster.

7 Wings for Victory campaign launched.

June 13 Germans drop first 'butterfly' bombs.

30 Churchill declares that German surrender must be unconditional.

July 29 Recruitment for women's services halted because more are needed for aircraft production.

September 24 Manpower crisis feared.

28 Italy surrenders.

October 29 Thames dockers on strike.

December 2 'Bevin Boys' sent to the mines.

1944

January 21 'Mini Blitz' strikes southern England.

February 1 Clothing restrictions lifted.

17 Government announces NHS plans.

24 Miners are given a 4-year pay deal.

April 27 All foreign travel banned.

30 Intensified Allied bombing campaign on communications in France.

June 5 D-Day: Allied troops land in Normandy.

June 13 First V-1 rockets ('doodlebugs') launched against London.

July 3 New evacuation of London begins as death toll from V-1 rockets increases.

    16 Reforms promised in new Education Act.

August 28 Only four of 94 V-1s get through because of new method of deflecting them.

September 6 Home Guard is partially stood down; blackout relaxed.

    17 'Dim-out' replaces blackout.

    18 First V-2 rockets launched.

October 8 New Ministry of Social Insurance formed.

    16 First British soldier demobilised.

November 20 Street lights turned on.

December 3 Farewell parade of the Home Guard.

1945

April 24 'Dim-out' abolished except in 5 coastal areas.

    30 Hitler commits suicide.

May 7 German High Command surrenders.

    8 Victory in Europe Day.

June 13 New family allowances scheme announced.

    18 Mass demobilisation begins.

July 5 General election held.

    26 Election result: landslide victory for Labour.

August 6 Atom bomb dropped on Hiroshima.

    9 Atom bomb dropped on Nagasaki.

    14 Japan surrenders.

    17 Labour announces social reform programme centred on NHS.

September 2 Press censorship ends.

November 5 Dockers' strike ends.

Index

CHERISHED LIBRARY BOMBED

'DAILY SKETCH' REPORTER

THE Cherished Library at Stanhope House, the ancestral home of the Cherish family, is believed to have been destroyed in a bombing raid on the evening of 23 May 1940. The collection comprised more than 1,500 rare books and parchments, many of which dated from the 16th century. After the fire had been quelled, volunteers moved in to save what they could from the smouldering ruins. Although hundreds of books were recovered, the fierce inferno carbonised a few hundred, rendering them unreadable. The Cherished Library is thought to have contained some surprises. The family were rumoured to be the custodians of the so-called 'Crypt Editions': journals, manuscripts, letters and books whose contents were deemed too shocking to be made available to the public at the time of their creation. An unverified account hints at the existence of Victor Frankenstein's Secret Journal on the workings of the human body.

FATEFUL RAID

THERE are two opposing accounts of the events that led to the destruction of the building that housed the Cherished Library at Stanhope House. Some evacuee children who saw the bombing say a British plane, hit by German fire, dropped its bombs on the mansion as it fell out of the sky. In another version, a neighbouring farmer maintains that a German pilot released his bombs over the Stanhope Estate on purpose, prompting other pilots in his formation to do the same. One of these bombs hit Stanhope House, causing the fire. A bomb also landed in the middle of the kitchen gardens and there was a shower of glass and debris from the greenhouses. Thankfully there were no casualties. At the beginning of hostilities in 1939, the precious books and manuscripts were moved from Molyneux House, the Cherish family's town house in London, to Stanhope, which had been deemed a safe location. The centrepiece of the collection is thought to have been the original manuscripts and research for a two-volume set of Scotland: A Very Peculiar History, by the distinguished historian Fiona Macdonald.

NAZI CAUGHT

A German pilot-lieutenant brought down in this country arrives at a South-East Coast railway station to entrain for a prisoner of war camp. His bombing days are over.